The Violent Take It BY FORCE

The Violent Take It BY FORCE

Intercession Made Easy

by

Prophetess Jackie Harewood

Unless otherwise noted, all Scripture quotations are from the Authorized King James Version of the Bible. References marked "NKJ" are from *The New King James Version of the Bible*, copyright © 1979, 1980, 1982, by Thomas Nelson, Inc., Nashville, Tennessee. References marked "AMP" are from *The Amplified Bible*, copyright © 1954, 1958, 1962, 1964, 1965, 1987 by The Lockman Foundation, La Habra, California. References marked "NIV" are from *The New International Version of the Bible,* copyright © 1973, 1978, 1984 by International Bible Society, Colorado Springs, Colorado. Portions marked "GNB" are from *The Good News Bible*, copyright © 1976 by the American Bible Society, New York, NY.
Word definitions are from the following sources: *New Strong's Exhaustive Concordance of the Bible*, copyright © 1984 by Thomas Nelson Publishers, Nashville and from the Libronix Digital Library System, including *Merriam-Webster's Collegiate Dictionary* (Eleventh Edition), *Greek-English Lexicon of the New Testament* Based on Semantic Domains and *Harper's Bible Dictionary*. A quotation in chapter 12 is from Earl Radmacher, Ronald B. Allen, and H. Wayne House, *Nelson's New Illustrated Bible Commentary* (Thomas Nelson, Inc. Publishers, 1990).

THE VIOLENT TAKE IT BY FORCE

Original cover design by Sherie Campbell
sonandshield@comcast.net

Published by:

McDougal & Associates
www.thepublishedword.com

McDougal & Associates is dedicated to the spreading of the Gospel of Jesus Christ to as many people as possible in the shortest time possible.

ISBN 13: 978-1-934769-11-9
ISBN 10: 1-934769-11-8

Printed in the United States of America
For Worldwide Distribution

Contents

And from the days of John the Baptist until now the kingdom of heaven suffereth violence, and the violent take it by force. Matthew 11:12

INTRODUCTION

As never before, in this hour God's Spirit is calling the Church to intercession, and His call is compelling. But what exactly is biblical intercession? What does it entail? How do we know what or who to intercede for? How long should we intercede? And what method should we use?

These are all important questions, but there is so much confusion out there about this subject that it's no wonder we're not getting better results in these days. If we don't even know what intercession is or how to go about it, how can we intercede effectively?

And that's the purpose of this book God's Spirit has laid upon my heart. In the coming pages, I want to lay out clearly and precisely, with the Spirit's help, the major truths we all need to know in order to become powerful intercessors in the days ahead. I will analyze the who, the what and the why of biblical intercession for the twenty-first century.

Intercession, as we shall see, is closely related to and interconnected with spiritual warfare. It is our privilege and duty to go forth and take back what the enemy has stolen—from us personally, from our families, our communities, our churches, our nation and our world.

The Violent Take It By Force. Will you be one of them?

Jackie Harewood
Baton Rouge, Louisiana

Part I

Definitions

Chapter 1

What Is Biblical Intercession?

And from the days of John the Baptist until now the kingdom of heaven suffereth violence, and the violent take it by force. Matthew 11:12

What is biblical intercession? It is "the act of mediation, entreaty, prayer or petition on behalf of someone other than yourself." In the Hebrew language, this word *intercession* is *paga,* which means "to impinge." To better understand the meaning of intercession, therefore, we must also understand the word *impinge.*

An intercessor violently takes action to enforce the will of God in the life of another!

Impinging on the Enemy's Territory

Impinge means "to strike against, hit upon, or dash something." It means "to collide with, to be violent against; to make inroads or encroach on or upon the property or rights of another; to drive in, or to invade." All of these definitions give the impression of violence. Therefore, we could say that an intercessor violently takes action to enforce the will of God in the life of another.

Jesus said that the Kingdom of Heaven *"suffers violence."* What does that mean? Those who are born again into the Kingdom of God become Kingdom citizens, heirs and joint heirs with Christ. As such, we have an avowed enemy. When the Word of God speaks of the Kingdom suffering violence, it refers to the work of our vicious opponent, the devil, and his associates. We, the Kingdom citizens, are violently treated and attacked by the devil on a regular basis. The apostle Paul wrote to the Church at Ephesus:

> *For we wrestle not against flesh and blood, but against principalities, against powers, against the rulers of the darkness of this world, against spiritual wickedness in high places.* Ephesians 6:12

This clearly indicates that the devil and his associates are organized against believers. A band of demonic, or sometimes even human, spirit soldiers are assigned to each individual promise that a believer eagerly awaits. Their job is to do all that they can to block its eventual fulfillment.

In Greek, the word translated *violent* is *biastes,* which stems from a root word meaning "energetic; to crowd oneself; to seize; press with force." When you come to understand that we serve a God who ignites a violent response in the heart of His believer and limits the violence of the opponent, you can better understand the important role of an intercessor.

Before the foundations of the world, the stage was set for the great battle, and after the Fall, God set the stage more fully. He said:

And I will put enmity between thee and the woman, and between thy seed and her seed; it shall bruise thy head, and thou shalt bruise his heel. Genesis 3:15

Ever since that fateful day, at the very dawn of civilization, intercessors have been bruising Satan's head. For his part, Satan has attacked everything dear to God's crowning creation, man, robbing and plundering him at every opportunity. But there is a spiritual power and strength that an intercessor can exert against the devil to regain the promises that God has for us. As intercessors, we are given power to control, persuade and influence the forces of darkness. An intercessor, then, enforces the will of God (beyond the natural limits and capacity to impose by force).

In the prayer that Jesus taught us, we pray:

Thy kingdom come. Thy will be done in earth, as it is in heaven. Matthew 6:10

An anointed intercessor brings God's will to earth, as it is in Heaven. The assignment of an intercessor, then, is to strike out against the enemy, to ensure that God's will is manifested on the Earth.

Encroaching on Enemy Territory

Another definition for *impinge* is "to encroach upon," which means "to enter by gradual steps or by slow, deliberate and secret action into the possession or rights of another; to advance beyond the usual or proper limits and invade the territory of the opponent." This is a wonderful definition, for it gives us a true picture of how we can recover what the devil has stolen from us.

"Slow, gradual steps" implies that intercession is a process that takes a deliberate action, forcibly moving the intercessor into the territory of the enemy, to regain the promises that were stolen.

Every intercessor has the authority to go beyond the natural, outside the reach, possibility and understanding of the carnal limits, and deal directly in the Spirit with the matter at hand. One called to intercede will meet with God in prayer, making an earnest request for His will to be done in a given situation and making it so by forcing back the enemy who opposes it.

The intercessor has an obligation to position himself between the perplexing difficult and the solution. He or she must war against the powers of darkness that resist God's will. Once the intercessor is in position, it is possible to grab hold of the answer, by using the Word of God and the gift of faith, to bridge the gulf of unanswered prayer. Isaiah declared:

> *And he saw that there was no man, and wondered that there was no intercessor: therefore his arm brought salvation unto him; and his righteousness, it sustained him.* Isaiah 59:16

No man had the ability to stand on behalf of another, but this phrase, *"His arm"* speaks of the Lord Jesus as a mighty warrior. When an intercessor stands, it is Jesus, the Heavenly Intercessor, who stands with him and for him.

As an intercessor exercises the authority given by Jesus to bring salvation to a hurting world, God's power is displayed through the believer, and he or she becomes an extension of the arm of God:

> *For he is not a man, as I am, that I should answer him, and we should come together in judgment. Neither is there any daysman betwixt us, that might lay his hand upon us both.* Job 9:32-33

This word *daysman* is also translated *umpire*. Job complained that God was not a man who would go to court with Him. And, Job also didn't have an impartial mediator between himself and God, someone who could present his case before the Almighty. An intercessor becomes just such a mediator and, thus, stands between God and humanity.

Who Can Be an Intercessor?

Intercessors are not strong in themselves, nor are they required to be spiritual giants. If you have a clean heart, are faithful to God and have a desire to be used by Him, you qualify. Our weaknesses and frailties never disqualify us from becoming spiritual warriors. To the contrary; in this way, God's strength is made perfect in our weakness:

And he [the Lord] said unto me [Paul], My grace is sufficient for thee: for my strength is made perfect in weakness. Most gladly therefore will I rather glory in my infirmities, that the power of Christ may rest upon me.

2 Corinthians 12:9

When the Lord called Gideon to lead the oppressed Israelites to victory against their oppressors, the Midianites, and take back what had been stolen from them, He told His servant Gideon why it didn't matter that he was not, at that moment, a mighty warrior:

And the LORD said unto Gideon, The people that are with thee are too many for me to give the Midianites into their hands, lest Israel vaunt themselves against me, saying, Mine own hand hath saved me.

Judges 7:2

God then went on to reduce the number of soldiers in Gideon's army from thirty-two thousand down to only three hundred. With an army that small, there could be no doubt that their victory had been given to them by God Himself. Such a small group of men could never take the credit for themselves.

Job didn't have an impartial mediator between himself and God, someone who could present his case before the Almighty!

Like Gideon, we must recognize that we can be confident of victory only if we put our trust in God and not in ourselves or our own abilities. We must recognize that in the eyes of the Lord the weak are strong, the rich are poor and the unlearned are learned. The unskilled become skilled in the hands of the Lord.

God's Word makes a wonderful statement about the weak and needy:

> *For the LORD will plead their cause and spoil the soul of those that spoiled them.* Proverbs 22:23

In other words, anyone who afflicts the defenseless makes an enemy of God, and He will take up their cause. How wonderful! It is to such causes that intercessors are called.

As an intercessor, God will always place a need in your heart. Then, as you are prompted to pray for that need, God will take up the cause. Because of your obedience to sacrifice your time to intercede for that situation, you become the instrument God uses to bring forth His will. And so, the battle is not yours to fight; it is the Lord's. However, He allows you to participate in the victory.

Taking Up the Cause of Others

Just as the Lord defends your personal cause, a believer called to be an intercessor can plead the cause of others before the Lord. That believer can plead with God, to persuade, to ask urgently, for another chance for a people or for a nation, much as Moses identified with and pleaded for the children of Israel.

Throughout history, God has never repented, but He has been known to show mercy at the request of His chosen intercessors:

> *Thus they provoked him to anger with their inventions: and the plague brake in upon them. Then stood up Phinehas, and executed judgment: and so the plague was stayed. And that was counted unto him for righteousness unto all generations for evermore.*
>
> Psalm 106:29-31

On this, as on many other occasions, God was provoked to anger by the children of Israel, and the result was that their priest, Phinehas, had to step in and intervene on their behalf. Phinehas later developed moral issues that ultimately caused him to lose his own life, but because of his being yielded to God to intercede for the people of Israel, he is remembered today. Intercession is more than just praying. It is standing for and becoming God's spokesman for a given situation.

Intercession Requires Commitment

Commitment is paramount in the life of an intercessor. The person who intercedes is one who is fully committed to prayer and to the service of God and others. Again, intercession is not just prayer; it is a way of life, one to which we are called.

Intercessors are placed in situations in which God can be glorified. For instance, being on a certain job can often mean the difference between life and death for some other person. Just the presence of that intercessor becomes an invitation for God to intervene in the lives of the men and women who work in that place. The place is blessed because of the presence of an anointed intercessor. Are you such a person?

Intercessors are placed in situations in which God can be glorified!

The presence of an intercessor brings the power of God into a situation. The fact that God's man or woman is there opens a door for Him to come on the scene. When a person is in need and no intercessor is around, that person may not be able to touch Heaven. But when an intercessor is present, God will be able to work on the situation, on the merit of the intercessor's having invited Him to intervene.

Intercessors Are Stirred Up

> *And there is none that calleth upon thy name, that stirreth up himself to take hold of thee; for thou hast hid thy face from us, and hast consumed us, because of our iniquities.* Isaiah 64:7

An intercessor must first stir himself up. This word *stirreth* comes from a Hebrew word that means "to be bare, to be made naked, to open the eyes, and to raise up thyself." To be bare and be made naked before the Lord is to be open, yielded and transparent. Only when your eyes are open in the spirit can you see the need at hand and pray the heart of God for another person.

The action of an intercessor is to rise up and to pursue the enemy in warfare. This is possible because intercessory prayer is the one power on earth that commands the power of Heaven. An intercessor has the ability to pray down the answer for others and, thus, defy all the existing powers of the world.

Of course, intercessors must learn to pray the will of God and not what they think is right for a given situation. Therefore, before praying a prayer of intercession, they must consult the Holy Spirit to learn what the will of the Father is. Effective intercessors live lives of contemplation and openness before God.

ENTREATY

In the New Testament, *intercession* is translated from a Greek word, *entusis,* which means, "a petition, supplication, and interview, to entreat and in favor or against." A petition is "an earnest request, a formal written request made to a superior; something asked or requested."

To present God with a written petition is something many intercessors have not yet done. Perhaps the time has come for every acceptable technique to be exercised.

It is acceptable to ask, and that asking can be done either in a verbal request or in written form. In making a written request, state your request as it relates to a promise, for God always watches over His Word to perform it (see Jeremiah 1:12). Then, as you write your petition and present it before the Father, make it known that you believe the Word of God to be true and that you expect God to watch over His Word to perform it.

Paul wrote to the Philippians:

> *Being confident of this very thing, that he which hath begun a good work in you will perform it until the day of Jesus Christ.* Philippians 1:6

We must be convinced that God will bring destiny to pass. How else can we pray with faith—for ourselves or for anyone else?

A petition is a reminder to God of His word, enforcing the authority of His Word against the resistance of the enemy and informing all interested parties that the will of God will be done in a specific situation.

The intercessor converses with God in an informal discussion of the issues being presented. In any conversation, there is always an exchange, and an interaction on the part of both parties. Therefore, time must be spent alone with God to obtain information as to His mind and will for this particular situation. As you converse with God, you will come into an awareness of His plan and the steps to be taken to arrive at the answer. He will then show you exactly what to do to bring it to pass.

CONCILIATION

Intercession is "an act between parties, with a view to reconcile differences of contention. To mediate, to plead, or interpose on behalf of another." Positionally, the intercessor becomes an intermediary or conciliator between God and man. Intervening on behalf of another becomes the posture:

> *And the fruit of righteousness is sown in peace of them that make peace.* James 3:18

Therefore, intercessors must guard their heart so that they will not become weary in well doing. Going to the Father in faith, knowing that we will be granted the will of the Father, is the venue that we have been assigned. And God has a special assignment for each and every intercessor. He will assign you special situations that you are to pray for and about. If your answer does not come right away, don't give up. Continue to press on in prayer:

> *And he said unto them, Which of you shall have a friend, and shall go unto him at midnight, and say unto him, Friend, lend me three loaves; for a friend of mine in his journey is come to me, ... and he shall answer and say, Trouble me not .... I cannot rise and give thee. I say unto you, Though he will not rise and give him, because he is his friend, yet because of his importunity he will rise and give him as many as he needeth.* Luke 11:5-8

This word *importunity* is defined as "shamefacelessness, to be unashamed, to have no pride, to continually ask even though it seems the person is unresponsive." That's the kind of intercessor God is searching for today. Will you hear His call?

The Violent Take It By Force. Will you be one of them?

Part II

Tools of Intercession

Chapter 2

Laughter

> *Abraham fell upon his face, and laughed, and said in his heart, Shall a child be born unto him that is an hundred years old? and shall Sarah, that is ninety years old, bear?* Genesis 17:17

In war, many strategies are employed. One of the surprising and often overlooked weapons that can be used in intercession is laughter.

Laughing in Scorn

There are different words used in the Bible for laughter. One of these is the Greek word *tsachaq,* and it means "to laugh outright in contempt, disdain, rejection or scorn, to mock and to make sport of." There is a sarcasm that you express when you laugh because you disbelieve something told to you, and you can use this technique against your enemy. When he whispers in your ear what he believes to be true, you can laugh at the fact and choose to believe what the Bible says about the situation instead.

Facts are facts, and they state the condition, but facts are also temporal and are subject to change at any given moment. God's Word is Truth and will never change. When you choose to believe His Word above the facts of your circumstances, therefore, His Truth about you will prevail.

When Jonah found himself in the belly of the whale, he made a relevant statement after he had cried to the Lord to help him out of his affliction. His statement was this:

They that observe lying vanities forsake their own mercy.

Jonah 2: 8

Jonah was saying that unless we can keep our eyes off of what we see, we will not believe in the mercy of God. So, what can we do? We must laugh at the facts and believe the truth.

The fact may be that your bills are due; the truth is that God will supply all your needs according to His riches in Christ Jesus (see Philippians 4:19). The fact may be that your marriage is falling apart; the truth is what God has put together let no man put asunder (see Matthew 19:6). The fact may be that your body is sick with a terminal disease; the truth is that by Jesus' stripes you are healed (see 1 Peter 2:24).

With Jonah, the situation didn't change immediately, but he believed that the facts would change, and they did. You, too, can believe God for His truth to come alive in your life, regardless of your circumstances. And that can enable you to laugh in the enemy's face.

Jonah was saying that unless we can keep our eyes off of what we see, we will not believe in the mercy of God!

Job knew what it was to be *"laughed to scorn,"* and he also knew what it was to do the laughing:

> *I am as one mocked of his neighbour, who calleth upon God, and he answereth him: the just upright man is laughed to scorn.* Job 12:4

> *At destruction and famine thou shalt laugh: neither shalt thou be afraid of the beasts of the earth.*
> Job 5:22

Laughing is such a powerful weapon, and you can use it just when the enemy thinks he has destroyed your blessings, caused you not to have enough money to run your household or when you're being threatened by others. Just laugh! Try it, and you'll be amazed at the results.

God Has a Sense of Humor

God, too, has a sense of humor, and this can be seen in the Scriptures. For instance, after Joseph's brothers had sold him into the hands of a foreign and pagan people, God caused those same brothers to have to come to him for help, and when they did, they felt compelled to bow before the very brother they had wronged:

> *And Joseph was the governor over the land, and he it was that sold to all the people of the land: and Joseph's brethren came, and bowed down themselves before him with their faces to the earth.* Genesis 42:6

Joseph could have laughed in that moment—if he hadn't been crying so much for the joy of seeing his brothers again.

Four hundred years later, Pharaoh planned to kill a child whom the prophets had spoken of. Because he was unsure of just which Hebrew child was the threat to his kingdom, he attempted to kill all of the Hebrew boy babies. But God delivered His chosen one by a very interesting plan. He was rescued by Pharaoh's daughter and raised in the palace at Pharaoh's expense. In this way, Moses enjoyed all of the best that Egypt had to offer.

How ironic! The man who attempted to kill Moses became his adoptive grandfather and educated Moses and lavished money on him for the very best in food and clothing:

> *And the child grew, and she brought him unto Pharaoh's daughter, and he became her son. And she called his name Moses: and she said, Because I drew him out of the water.* Exodus 2:10

Who but our God could cause such a thing to happen?

In another Old Testament twist of fate, the evil Haman was hanged on the very gallows he had erected for the hated Jew Mordecai:

> *So they hanged Haman on the gallows that he had prepared for Mordecai. Then was the king's wrath pacified.* Esther 7:10

Haman thought he was the man about to be honored, but the tables turned on him and all that he had wished for himself was done instead for the man he hated so much. God will bring great embarrassment to those who humiliate you. He said:

Haman thought he was the man about to be honored, but the tables turned on him!

The wicked plotteth against the just .... The Lord shall laugh at him: for he seeth that his day is coming.
Psalm 37:12-13

Swords are in their lips: for who, say they, doth hear? But thou, O LORD, *shalt laugh at them; thou shalt have all the heathen in derision.* Psalm 59:7-8

He that sitteth in the heavens shall laugh: the Lord shall have them in derision. Psalm 2:4

God laughs, and you can too.

Abraham Laughed Uncontrollably

As we noted in the text verse for this chapter, the words of the Lord made Abraham laugh so hard that he lost complete control of himself, fell on his face, lay prostrate on the ground and shook with laughter. Let's look at a little more of the context of that incident:

And God said unto Abraham, As for Sarai thy wife, thou shalt not call her name Sarai, but Sarah shall her name be. And I will bless her, and give thee a son also of her: yea, I will bless her, and she shall be a mother of nations; kings of people shall be of her. Then Abraham fell upon his face, and laughed, and said in his heart, Shall a child be born unto him that is an hundred years old? and shall Sarah, that is ninety years old, bear? Genesis 17:15-17

The time will come when God will give us promises that will seem just as ridiculous and absurd as these promises seemed to Abraham, and if our faith is strong, we, too, will laugh. There are times when the enemy will throw himself against us so fiercely that we will despair of life. Still, if we believe God, we can laugh in those moments.

God wants His people to have a sense of humor and to use it against the enemy and his plans. He wants us to laugh at our debts, our sicknesses, our dried-up bodies, our many enemies, our dry pastures, our old age and every other difficult situation in our lives and in the lives of those for whom we are called to intercede. We can literally laugh our way to victory.

LAUGHTER IS LIKE A MEDICINE

Laughter, the Scriptures declare, is like a medicine:

A merry heart doeth good like a medicine: but a broken spirit drieth the bones. Proverbs 17:22

Laughter will actually lengthen your days on the earth and, conversely, a lack of it will shorten them.

The word that is translated here as *drieth* is *yabesh*, from a word that means "to dry up, confuse, confound, shame, wither away." The word translated *bones* is *etsem*, and it means "the body, the strength, the bones." Thus, a merry heart will strengthen, heal and give you stamina, but a broken spirit confuses, confounds, shames, withers away and dries up the body and its strength. This is serious, and we all need to take heed.

Abraham was not the only one to laugh; Sarah also received this gift of laughter from the Lord:

Therefore Sarah laughed within herself.

Genesis 18:12

Many people lose their strength because they lose their joy. That's why the Word of the Lord says:

Sara herself received strength to conceive seed.

Hebrews 11:11

During the time of King Hezekiah, the great warrior king, Sennacherib of the Assyrians, threatened to come against the city of Jerusalem. He actually wrote a very threatening and mocking letter personally addressed and personally hand-delivered to Hezekiah. When the king read it, he was in great consternation. What should he do? In his dismay, he went into the house of the Lord and spread that threatening letter before God. In response, the Lord sent a message to Hezekiah through Isaiah the prophet. To Hezekiah's surprise, this is what God had to say about the feared enemy, Sennacherib, and his mocking threats:

> *This is the word that the LORD hath spoken concerning him; The virgin the daughter of Zion hath despised thee, and laughed thee to scorn; the daughter of Jerusalem hath shaken her head at thee.* 2 Kings 19:21

"The daughters of Zion" mentioned here were intercessors who used laughter against their enemies. You, too, can laugh your enemy to scorn. It works.

In this case, God saw into the future and knew just what would happen, and so He announced it as if it were a thing that had already happened. And that's what He longs for us to do too. We must look into His finished work and see His answer to our prayer and envision things as they will be when He has finished working out every problem and every situation which is threatening us and those for whom we intercede at this very moment. There is power in this kind of laughter.

LAUGHTER IS HOLY

We have come to the laughter that results from allowing God's Spirit to do a sovereign work in us, relieving us of our sorrows and burdens and injecting us with heavenly joy as "holy laughter," and so it is. When we laugh at God's victory over evil and see the humor in the everyday situations of life, that's a holy act. And God loves it. After all, if God can speak through us, He can also laugh through us.

He said:

A time to weep, and a time to laugh. Ecclesiastes 3:4

The righteous also shall see, and fear, and shall laugh at him. Psalm 52:6

By faith we see the imminent power of the final workings of God, and as we have respect and reverence for Him, we can then laugh at the enemy and put him in his place.

Again, Job declared:

Behold, God will not cast away a perfect man, neither will he help the evildoers: Till he fill thy mouth with laughing, and thy lips with rejoicing. Job 8:20-21

You will have a good laugh when you finally see what God will do with your enemy. Our God will not cast you away, and neither will He help the evildoer who threatens you so mercilessly:

Then was our mouth filled with laughter, and our tongue with singing: then said they among the heathen, The LORD hath done great things for them.
Psalm 126:2

The moment we begin to laugh, it will be a great witness before all men, believers and non-believers alike. It will prove to them the great confidence which we have in our God.

The Violent Take It By Force. Will you be one of them?

Chapter 3

Praise

Now will I praise the LORD. Genesis 29:35

It's interesting to note that the first person mentioned in the Bible as having praised the Lord was a woman—Leah, the despised and rejected wife of Jacob. She had borne him three sons already, and still he couldn't find it in his heart to love her.

The first person mentioned in the Bible as having praised the Lord was a woman—Leah, the despised and rejected wife of Jacob!

Discovering What Praise Can Do

When their first son had been born, Leah named him Reuben, because she said:

Surely the LORD hath looked upon my affliction; now therefore my husband will love me.
Genesis 29:32

Unfortunately, it didn't happen. When their second son came along, Leah named him Simeon, for she said:

Because the LORD hath heard that I was hated, he hath therefore given me this son also. Genesis 29:33

This also didn't seem to help. When a third son was born to this dismal union, Leah named him Levi, for she said:

> *Now this time will my husband be joined unto me, because I have born him three sons.* Genesis 29:34

But still her husband took very little notice of her. It wasn't until the fourth son was born that Leah learned the secret of unlocking the heart of God. She named this son Judah, which means "praise." She had determined in her heart:

> *Now will I praise the LORD.* Genesis 29:35

After Judah was born, for the time being, Leah stopped having children. She hadn't yet seen all of her desires visited upon Jacob, her reluctant husband, but she was content anyway. From that moment on, she would praise the Lord, and He would fight her battles for her. She hadn't been doing very well on her own.

As a result of her love for the Lord and her willingness to praise Him even in difficult times, Leah outlived her younger sister by many years. It was Leah who had the honor of having her husband buried at her side (see Genesis 49:31). She and Jacob spent their latter years together.

PRAISE IS A POWERFUL TOOL

Praise is a tool that will open gates for the one who will dare to use it. As Isaiah declared:

Violence shall no more be heard in thy land, wasting nor destruction within thy borders; but thou shalt call thy walls Salvation, and thy gates Praise. Isaiah 60:18

You will find that, as you praise the Lord, doors will open in walls where there were no doors before, and you will be able to come out of your imprisonment and confinement through these doors of praise. You can walk out of lack, depression, loneliness, despair and poverty if you will only learn to use praise as a weapon. And if you can do it for yourself personally, then you can do it for others in intercession.

When Paul and Silas were imprisoned in Philippi, they began to praise the Lord. The impact of their praise was so mighty that it caused a great earthquake, and that earthquake shook the very foundations of the prison, so that immediately all the doors were opened. Their praise was so powerful that it affected all those around them. All of the prisoners' bands were loosed, not just their own (see Acts 16:25-26). This is such an important point.

Their praise not only opened the prison doors, but it also shook the chains off of their arms and legs. And you, too, can praise the Lord to get loose from your bondages and bad habits and then to see others set free as well.

Praise God in the Presence of Demons

There are times when the devil and his host just need to hear your voice of praise. You will make them uncomfortable when you praise the Lord in their presence:

O bless our God, ye people, and make the voice of his praise to be heard. Psalm 66:8

It is clear that God expects to hear our voice when we praise Him, and if He hears it, so does the enemy.

Praise always accompanies revival. For every revival recorded, God has given a song to His people. During the time of Hezekiah's revival, for example, he appointed priests and Levites to give thanks and to praise in the openings of the tents of the Lord (see 2 Chronicles 31:2). God also wants you to praise Him, not only in His house, but also in your tents, your dwelling places, in your house or wherever you find yourself. This is also true of anyplace God sends you to intercede for others.

He does admonish us:

Praise him in the assembly of the elders.
Psalm 107:32

So never be afraid or ashamed to lift up your voice in praise in the congregation of the people. But God not only encourages us to praise Him in front of men; He also wants us to praise Him in the presence of demons and in the presence of every evil circumstance of life.

On many occasions the psalmist showed this:

I will praise thee with my whole heart: before the gods will I sing praise unto thee. Psalm 138:1

The gods are representatives of demon spirits and

fallen angels. When we praise the Lord in front of demon spirits, we are truly engaged in effective warfare, the outcome of which, will be victory for us and those we stand for and certain defeat for the enemy who harasses us all.

Put on "the Garment of Praise"

There is a garment of praise that we can be clothed in. Isaiah mentioned it:

> *To give unto them beauty for ashes, the oil of joy for mourning, the garment of praise for the spirit of heaviness.*
>
> Isaiah 61:3

We must put off the garments of mourning and complaining, fault-finding, criticism, and self-pity, and put on, instead, this garment of praise. It is important for intercessors to have joy. You can never give joy to someone else as long as you yourself are wearing the garment of mourning. When we are encouraged and walking in victory, then and only then, can we encourage others.

We can only give what we have. So, if we have joy, we can give joy to others. If all we have is sadness, then sadness is all that we can give away. If all we have is heaviness, then heaviness is all that we can give away. Put on the garment of praise today.

Give "the Sacrifice of Praise"

Even in Old Testament times, a sacrifice of praise was expected on the part of God's people:

And they shall come from the cities of Judah, and from the places about Jerusalem, and from the land of Benjamin, and from the plain, and from the mountains, and from the south, bringing burnt offerings, and sacrifices, and meat offerings, and incense, and bringing sacrifices of praise, unto the house of the LORD.

Jeremiah 17:26

We must put off the garments of mourning and complaining, fault-finding, criticism and self-pity, and put on, instead, this garment of praise!

This has not changed in New Testament times. A sacrifice of praise is still expected in the house of the Lord. The difference between the Old Testament sacrifice and the New Testament sacrifice is that the old was actually a physical act, while the new is a spiritual act. Our praise should outshine the worship of the Old Testament as much as the perfect sacrifice of the New Testament outshines the bulls and goats of that older period.

The writer of the Hebrews said:

Let us offer the sacrifice of praise to God continually, that is, the fruit of our lips giving thanks to his name.

Hebrews 13:15

Every time we begin to speak of how we are thankful to God for the many blessings He has given us, we send up a spiritual sacrifice. Every time we do good, it ascends as a sweet smelling sacrifice to God.

But a sacrifice is something that costs you something. Let your lips be the sacrificial lamb that is laid upon the altar in thanksgiving and gratitude, and you will go away rejoicing and bringing victory to yourself and to others.

Even the poor and needy are exhorted to praise the Lord:

> *Let the poor and needy praise thy name.*
>
> Psalm 74:21

Do people who are poor and needy have anything to praise God about? Of course they do. And, when you praise the Lord in the midst of want and need, God begins to multiply that which you have, and you will be amazed at the outcome. So learn to use praise as a weapon against every evil force that assails you and those you are assigned to fight for.

The Violent Take It By Force. Will you be one of them?

Chapter 4

Upraised Hands

Hear the voice of my supplications, when I cry unto thee, when I lift up my hands toward thy holy oracle.

Psalm 28:2

There are many ways in which we praise God, and one of them is by raising our hands to Him. There is tremendous power in the simple act of offering upraised hands to the Almighty. We lift up our hands because we reverence and acknowledge Him and the *"Holy Oracle."*

This phrase, *"the holy oracle,"* referred to the holy commandments, or the Holy Word of God, which was given to His people. In the Old Testament, when the people prayed, they reached their hands out toward the Holy Ark of the Covenant. Now, our focus is different, for now, in this time, the Word has been made flesh:

And the Word was with God, and the Word was God. ... And the Word was made flesh, and dwelt among us, (and we beheld his glory, the glory as of the only begotten of the Father,) full of grace and truth.

John 1:1 and 14

Jesus Christ became the revealed Word of God to us. He is the Holy Oracle today. The original Holy Oracle was merely a type of the Christ to come. Christ has risen from the dead and ascended to the right hand of God, and that is why, when we worship Him, we raise our hands upward, for we are raising them toward the Holy Oracle—just as the Israelites did in David's time. We don't look for God at eye-level, but we raise our hands and look above, because Jesus is seated in the heavens with the Father.

PORTRAYING HUMILITY AND SURRENDER

Lifting our hands allows our very body to enter the act of worship. Did you realize that your body performs acts that portray your emotions? When you raise your hands, you portray humility, and you portray total surrender and dependence upon God. When you stand up for God, you portray readiness to serve, to go on or continue in His will.

> ***Lifting our hands allows our very body to enter the act of worship!***

God told the Israelites of Moses' day that they were to eat the Passover meal standing. This portrayed a readiness to march, to advance, to take a chance at going on to higher heights and deeper depths in the Lord. When you sit down, it portrays rest and trust in the Lord.

Every act that your body performs is clearly a demonstration of particular emotions. Dancing, for instance, expresses great joy. When you lift up your hands, it is an act of body worship, which means that you are letting God know, with your whole body, how much you love

Him. Lifting your hands to God, therefore, becomes *"as the evening sacrifice"*:

> *Let my prayer be set forth before thee as incense; and the lifting up of my hands as the evening sacrifice.*
>
> Psalm 141:2

Drawing Heaven's Attention

When you lift your hands to God, you draw attention to yourself. Heaven starts to look your way. All the heavenly hosts have their eyes on you. When you lift your hands, you identify yourself as being the proper target for the blessings of God. How many other people in your city do you suppose are lifting their hands in worship to God at that moment? Probably not many. So, you're setting yourself up for a blessing.

God is always pleased to see His children waving holy hands up to Him. He delights in seeing your hands lifted in a gesture that implies, "Here I am, Lord, standing in the need of prayer."

In lifting your hands, you will not only draw the attention of the armies of Heaven to yourself; you also will connect with Heaven's high voltage power line and set yourself up for a heavenly hook-up.

Many Other Powerful Passages

There are many other wonderful scriptures that

speak of the power of uplifted hands to God. Here are a few more:

Lift up your hands in the sanctuary, and bless the LORD.
Psalm 134:2

Because thy lovingkindness is better than life, my lips shall praise thee.
Thus will I bless thee while I live: I will lift up my hands in thy name. Psalm 63:3-4

I will therefore that men pray every where, lifting up holy hands, without wrath and doubting.
1 Timothy 2:8

Wherefore lift up the hands which hang down, and the feeble knees. Hebrews 12:12

Clearly this is an effective tool of intercession that we all need to be using.
The Violent Take It By Force. Will you be one of them?

Chapter 5

Walking or Marching

Arise, walk through the land in the length of it and in the breadth of it; for I will give it unto thee.

Genesis 13:17

> ***There can be no doubt that there is a certain miraculous power connected with walking or marching in praise!***

There can be no doubt that there is a certain miraculous power connected with walking or marching in praise, especially when we do it over property that God has promised to us. This particular verse was directed to Abraham, but others received similar instructions in their time.

The Key to Possession

When God told Abraham to walk through the land of the Canaanites, He was giving him the key to possession of it. If you want to possess, just walk or march through the land. And God was also showing us how to claim that which He wants to give us and those for whom we are placed to intercede.

In Abraham's case, he did what God commanded him, and yet it was more than four hundred years later when the land finally came into the possession of His descendants. That doesn't mean you will have to wait four hundred years for your promise, but we must all heed the words of the prophet:

> *For the vision is yet for an appointed time, but at the end it shall speak, and not lie: though it tarry, wait for it; because it will surely come, it will not tarry.*
>
> Habakkuk 2:3

God never forgot the covenant He had made with Abraham. Generations later, He spoke to Joshua to place his anointed feet on the very same land:

> *There shall not any man be able to stand before thee all the days of thy life: as I was with Moses, so I will be with the: I will not fail thee, nor forsake thee.*
>
> Joshua 1:5

God was saying to Joshua: "When you walk the land, as the soles of your feet touch the soil, you are staking out your claim." And, just as much land remained for Joshua and his people to possess, we can certainly say that, in these last days, much land remains to be possessed by us as well. For too long, we have allowed the enemy to usurp authority over the rightful owners, the true citizens of the Kingdom. The day has come when the Lord wants us to rise up and possess our inheritance.

POSSESSION DEMANDS COURAGE

These, words spoken to Joshua in his day of possession, have rung out through the ages:

Only be thou strong and very courageous, that thou mayest observe to do according to all the law, which Moses my servant commanded thee: turn not from it to the right hand or to the left, that thou mayest prosper whithersoever thou goest. Joshua 1:7

It's time for us to take a walk with God and stake out our claim. It's time to walk over the territory that is rightfully ours and claim it. We must never forget our God-given right and imperative to take the land. When we rise up and stake it out, that releases God to give it to us as an inheritance.

Zechariah's Vision

The prophet Zechariah had an interesting vision (see Zechariah 6:1-8). He saw four chariots pulled by horses going out in the direction of the four winds. When he did not understand what the vision meant, an angel explained to him:

These are the four spirits of the heavens, which go forth from standing before the Lord of all the earth.
Zechariah 6:5

The four spirits, represented by four horses, were to *"walk to and fro through the earth"* at the Lord's command (Verse 7). The reason is revealed in the very next verse:

Behold, these that go toward the north country have quieted my spirit in the north country.
Zechariah 6:8

The next time there's trouble in your church, in your household, on your job or in your ministry, or trouble you are sent to handle for others, why not try walking the territory and claiming God's Spirit to quiet the place and bring peace? Drive out the evil spirits from that territory.

In Zechariah's case, God sent the messengers of peace into the North country because Israel's enemies often came from that direction. God knows where your enemies are, and He will send out His cavalry to quiet things down for you, if you'll just walk the land at His command.

WALK ABOUT ZION

In the Psalms, God instructs us:

Walk about Zion, and go round about her: tell the towers thereof. Psalm 48:12

This word *tell* is translated from the Hebrew *iscaphar*, which means, "to score with a mark, as a tally, or record, to inscribe, to enumerate, to celebrate, to count, to declare, to show forth." God rejoices when His people take another look at the great things He has done for them. Walk around your community and declare the blood of the Lamb. Walk around your job site and welcome the dealings of the Spirit of God there. Declare the blessings of God on everything and everyone around you.

When Ruth, the Moabitess arrived in Bethlehem, she was nothing but a widowed beggar, the poorest of the poor, and she went out to glean in the fields of Boaz. This meant simply that she went to see if she could find any grains dropped by the harvesters or any ripe grain accidently left standing by them. But as she walked through those fields, she was making the first steps in claiming them as her own. Ruth didn't realize, as she went out to glean in the fields, that a son who would come from her womb would be the next owner of the very fields she gleaned.

When we walk to and fro throughout any land, we are claiming the territory for God, and we are pushing the enemy back:

> *Thou hast put all things in subjection under his feet.*
>
> Hebrews 2:8

Christ is in us, and therefore, all things are under our feet, when He lives in and through our lives.

The Word of the Lord to you today is this:

> *Arise, walk through the land in the length of it and in the breadth of it; for I will give it unto thee.*
>
> Genesis 13:17

Believe it and act on it today, for personal victories and for victories in your ministry of intercession for others.

The Violent Take It By Force. Will you be one of them?

Chapter 6

Clapping Or Stomping

O clap your hands, all ye people; shout unto God with the voice of triumph. Psalm 47:1

Clapping your hands is another effective weapon for victory. It can have different meanings. It may mean that you are expressing joy, or that you are expressing either disdain or appreciation. You could be applauding someone or you could be mocking someone. You could be clapping to encourage someone or simply to greet someone.

Clapping Denotes Appreciation

It is scriptural for God's people to clap their hands to Him in appreciation for His greatness and His goodness. The Scriptures state that even creation claps its hands:

Let the floods clap their hands: let the hills be joyful together. Psalm 98:8

For ye shall go out with joy, and be led forth with peace: the mountains and the hills shall break forth before you into singing, and all the trees of the field shall clap their hands. Isaiah 55:12

Our word *clap* is translated from the Hebrew *macha*, which means "to rub, to strike the hands together in exultation, to clap." It is an act of triumph, jubilation and rejoicing. When we go forth in joy, we cause our joy to fall upon creation around us. Soon the very creation of God, the trees, respond to our happiness. The creation, in its own way, exalts the Lord in jubilation.

Clapping Can Also Denote Disdain

Clapping can also be used to express disdain, scorn, haughtiness and contempt:

> *All that pass by clap their hands at thee.*
>
> Lamentations 2:15

In ancient times, clapping was a sign of mockery and scorn, as when the people clapped their hands at Jerusalem.

> ***Clapping is an act of triumph, jubilation and rejoicing!***

Therefore, when the Lord calls us to clap our hands, it can have two purposes. (1) It praises and applauds the Lord, and (2) It mocks at the devil and his evil spirits. I find this to be very wonderful. It's a double whammy!

Clapping As Part of Spiritual Warfare

In some ancient oriental customs, priests and idol worshippers clapped their hands at funerals, in temples and other places of worship, recognizing that clapping the hands chased devils away. Clapping was one aspect of spiritual warfare, even in Bible times:

> *Thus saith the Lord God; Smite with thine hand, and stamp with thy foot, and say, Alas for all the evil abomination of the house of Israel! for they shall fall by the sword, by the famine, and by the pestilence.*
>
> Ezekiel 6:11

God was telling the prophet Ezekiel to act out the judgment that was about to come upon Israel because of her sins. It is scriptural, therefore, to *"smite with [the] hand"* or clap, and to *"stamp with [the] foot,"* or stomp our feet, against the enemy. Try it. You'll be blessed.

The Violent Take It By Force. Will you be one of them?

Chapter 7

Waiting

Wait on the Lord: be of good courage, and he shall strengthen thine heart: wait, I say, on the Lord.

Psalm 27:14

One of the most overlooked weapons that we have at our disposal which can be used for intercession is waiting. Waiting? A weapon? Yes, waiting is a powerful weapon against any enemy.

> ***In this life, we must all wait. We have no choice!***

Everyone Must Wait

In this life, we must all wait. We have no choice. God has a timing for all the events of your life, and since He alone controls the flow of events, nothing happens before He wants it to happen. More of us need to be able to understand His timing.

The Scriptures speak of the children of Issachar who *"had understanding of the times"*:

And of the children of Issachar, which were men that had understanding of the times, to know what Israel ought to do; the heads of them were two hundred; and all their brethren were at their commandment.

1 Chronicles 12:32

This word *time* is translated from a Hebrew word

koros, which means God's perfect timing. God has our lives sequenced with the universe. We must be able to handle the answer we are believing Him for, and everything else must line up in order to cause all things to work together for our good and the good of those around us. And, since those elements are all complex, only God knows that perfect timing.

WAITING REQUIRES COURAGE

In the meantime, we must remain in a position of waiting, if we're expecting an answer to our prayers. Regardless of our eagerness to get our answer immediately, many times we have to wait. That's just the way God does things.

When David said, *"Wait on the Lord,"* he was giving God's mandate for each of us. Whether we like it or not, we are instructed to *"wait."* And yet waiting is, perhaps, the most difficult activity assigned to the believer. Courage is essential to having an ability to wait for just the right time.

The word *wait* is used many times in the book of Psalms because David found himself in many trying and seemingly impossible situations. We can observe his life and determine that if we are successful in our waiting on the Lord, it will prove to be very productive for us, as it did for him.

But, again, waiting is never easy. David gives us a very clear picture of what it was like for him:

I am weary of my crying: my throat is dried: mine eyes fail while I wait for my God. Psalm 69:3

Many would agree with this anatomy of waiting.

The Process of Waiting

There is a physical response to waiting, as well as a spiritual aspect. Waiting is a process:

Behold, as the eyes of servants look unto the hand of their masters, and as the eyes of a maiden unto the hand of her mistress; so our eyes wait upon the LORD our God, until that he have mercy upon us. Psalms 123:2

To wait honorably is to look with expectation and with complete dependency upon God to provide the answer. The psalmist declared:

The eyes of all wait upon thee; and thou givest them their meat in due season. Thou openest thine hand, and satisfiest the desire of every living thing.

Psalm 145:15-16

Our eyes look to the One who holds the solution in His power, and we must trust that He will release the answer at the appointed time. Again, hear the words of David:

I wait for the LORD, my soul doth wait, and in his word do I hope. My soul waiteth for the LORD more than they that watch for the morning: I say, more than they that watch for the morning. Psalm 130:5-6

When one speaks of the soul waiting, it emphasizes the necessity of our entire being becoming involved in the process. It is just as Jesus taught:

Jesus said unto him, Thou shalt love the Lord thy God with all thy heart, and with all thy soul, and with all thy mind. This is the first and great commandment.
Matthew 22:37-38

This speaks of a totality of participation in the waiting process. When we consider intellect, mind, will and emotions, we are speak of a total person and that total person must remain in the depths of waiting for as long as it takes until the time is right.

AS ONE WAITS FOR THE MORNING

David spoke of waiting as one waits for the morning. What did he mean by that? Night has always been a time that amplifies pain, sickness and distress. It seems that in physical darkness anything contrary to the light has a greater influence.

For instance, people sin more boldly at night. Jesus said:

And this is the condemnation, that light is come into the world, and men loved darkness rather than light, because their deeds were evil. For every one that doeth evil hateth the light, neither cometh to the light, lest his deeds should be reproved. John 3:19-20

True believers wait, knowing that there is a freedom in light, and light comes with the morning hours. The promises of God's Word become our hope as we wait with great anticipation.

Hope, the Primary Ingredient of Waiting

Hope is the primary ingredient for waiting:

Let Israel hope in the LORD*: for with the* LORD *there is mercy, and with him is plenteous redemption.*
Psalm 130:7

Israel had such a hope, and we must have it too.

The Connection Between Waiting and Praise

David declared:

Praise waiteth for thee, O God, in Zion: and unto thee shall the vow be performed. Psalm 65:1

Praise, as we have noted earlier in the book, is a strategic weapon that can be used to defeat the enemy, and it is tied to waiting:

Let the high praises of God be in their mouth, and a two-edged sword in their hand; to execute vengeance upon the heathen, and punishments upon the people; to bind their kings with chains, and their nobles with fetters of iron; to execute upon them the judgment written: this honour have all this saints. Praise ye the LORD.

Psalm 149:6-9

True believers wait, knowing that there is a freedom in light, and light comes with the morning hours!

As we exercise our God-given right to praise God with our lips, our praise becomes like a sword. That sword renders conviction of sin on the nonbeliever and conviction of unrighteousness on the Christian who is not in right standing with God. It also binds Satan and his demons and pulls down strongholds.

The most interesting thing to note here is the relationship between praise and waiting: *"praise waiteth for thee."* It is comforting to know that when we praise, that praise ascends into Heaven and is constantly there in the presence of God. It is there to remind Him of your allegiance and your need. It pleases the Father to receive such praise, and it then becomes a perpetual memorial before Him.

Cornelius Built a Memorial Before God

Cornelius of New Testament fame was a Roman centurion, one who was part of a regiment of the Roman military. A Roman legion numbered about six thousand men, and each legion had ten cohorts of about six hundred men each. These cohorts were then divided into centuries of a hundred men each, and each century was commanded by a centurion, something like a modern sergeant. Cornelius was a Gentile of Italian descent, and he and his family were God-fearing:

> *There was a certain man in Caesarea called Cornelius, a centurion of the band called the Italian band, a devout man, and one that feared God with all his house, which gave much alms to the people, and prayed to God alway. He saw in a vision evidently about the ninth hour of the day an angel of God coming in to him, and saying unto him, Cornelius. And when he looked on him, he was afraid, and said, What is it, Lord? And he said unto him, Thy prayers and thine alms are come up for a memorial before God. And now send men to Joppa, and call for one Simon, whose surname is Peter: He lodgeth with one Simon a tanner, whose house is by the sea side: he shall tell thee what thou oughtest to do.* Acts 10:1-6

Cornelius' prayers and giving became a memorial before God. Arising like incense in the temple, the prayers and giving of all sincere seekers are effective and erect a monument, or statue, of sorts, before God.

When you take a vacation and visit some interesting area, there are usually some statues or monuments of interest to see. They remind us of some great person or event. In the same way, every time you express a word or gesture of praise, that praise ascends into Heaven, and then it makes its way to a designated place in the presence of the Lord, a place the Holy Ghost has reserved for it to stand. And there it waits. The more you praise, the grander and higher your statue becomes in the presence of the Lord.

I can't help but think that, as God goes about His everyday business, He can't help but remember you. When He turns to the left or to the right, your memorial will ever be before Him. What a great impression we make upon God as He sees our praise mounting up before Him and just waiting there!

There is little else we can offer God, but He is so intent upon receiving our praise that He will even delay wrath and preserve you so that He can receive it:

> *For my own name's sake I delay my wrath; for the sake of my praise I hold it back from you, so as not to cut you off.* Isaiah 48:9, NIV

Now, Let Us Turn Our Attention to Heaven

Now, let us turn our attention to Heaven:

Our praise, in a similar way, makes a monument to remind God of our faithfulness, our present need and our dependency on Him to answer all our needs!

And I saw the seven angels which stood before God; and to them were given seven trumpets. And another angel was given ... much incense, that he should offer it with the prayers of all saints upon the golden altar which was before the throne. And the smoke of the incense, which came with the prayers of the saints, ascended up before God out of the angel's hand. Revelation 8:2-4

These seven angels who are mentioned as standing before God are the angels of the seven churches. This is a picture of our prayers becoming a sweet savor and a pleasant aroma to Him. Our praise, in a similar way, makes a monument to remind God of our faithfulness, our present need and our dependency on Him to answer all our needs.

Staying in Place

When David wrote the words, *"Praise waiteth for thee,"* (Psalm 65:1), *Strong's* denotes this word *wait* as meaning "stillness from activity; to be dumb or silent; to fail to perish and to fail to be destroyed." *Stillness* denotes "to stay in a place, to remain inactive in anticipation until something expected takes place, remaining inactive with great expectation and anticipation until the answer to your prayer is manifested." When we speak of stillness, it's a picture of our praise remaining inactive in anticipation and refusing to move from the presence of God.

As our praise waits on Him, so do our prayers. They both stands in the presence of God with great anticipation, eager to see the answer come into fruition. Our praise waits right there patiently until what is expected takes place.

Praise leaves our heart, enters the presence of the Lord and then just stands there in the stillness of eternity until the answer comes. This is one of the reasons that Satan works so hard to prevent praise. He knows what a great weapon it is. It defeats him in the present, and it serves as a continual reminder to God that you are waiting on your breakthrough. Every time you praise God you make a determination toward your victory and the victory of those for whom you intercede.

The Violent Take It By Force. Will you be one of them?

Chapter 8

Repenting

Then tell them that the Lord has said, "Your ancestors turned away from me and worshiped and served other gods. They abandoned me and did not obey my teachings. But you have done even worse than your ancestors. All of you are stubborn and evil, and you do not obey me. So then, I will throw you out of this land into a land that neither you nor your ancestors have ever known." Jeremiah 16:11-13, GNB

Repentance is a spiritual principle increasingly being taught and practiced in the world prayer movement as a key to advancing the Gospel. Repenting opens the door for revival in every nation, city and people group on earth.

Identification Repentance

The precise tactic being employed is better known as Identification Repentance. It is basically a prayer, but this prayer asks God to release us and others from the consequences and satanic oppression caused by past and present sins, not necessarily our own. Hosea said:

They ask for revelations from a piece of wood! A stick tells them what they want to know! They have left me. Like a woman who becomes a prostitute, they have given themselves to other gods. At sacred places on the mountaintops they offer sacrifices, and on the hills they burn incense under tall, spreading trees, because the shade is so pleasant! As a result, your daughters serve as prostitutes, and your daughters-in-laws commit adultery. Hosea 4:12-13, GNB

Exodus 34:5-7, 20:5-6 and parallel Old Testament passages such as Leviticus 18:25, Deuteronomy 5:9 and others teach that it is the Lord's heart and character to show compassion and love toward the generations of those who love Him. Still, His holiness also causes Him to *"visit the iniquity"* of parents upon their descendants to the third and fourth generation.

Repentance is a spiritual principle increasingly being taught and practiced in the world prayer movement!

The Hebrew word *avon* primarily denotes iniquity as a state of guilt. It means that parental sin patterns and sin guilt will be visited upon, repaid to or measured out upon the children (Isaiah 65:6-7 and Jeremiah 32:18). (For more on this subject of iniquity, see Chapter 10.) In other words, children will *not* be punished for their parents' sins, but they will be influenced by the sin weaknesses, sin tendencies and spiritual bondage of their parents, and they may well fall prey to the same or similar sins.

In support of this, Jeremiah said:

Our fathers have sinned, and are not; and we have borne their iniquities.

The crown is fallen from our head: woe unto us, that we have sinned! Lamentations 5:7 and 16

They are turned back to the iniquities of their forefathers, which refused to hear my words; and they went after other gods to serve them: the house of Israel and the house of Judah have broken my covenant which I made with their fathers. Jeremiah 11:10

The implicit challenge to the children in these passages, made explicit in Ezekiel 18:20 and Jeremiah 31:29-30, is to repent and make a break with parental and generational sin, rather than continue in it. Some Old Testament scholars suggest that such transference of iniquity and guilt and the deferring of full judgment from one generation to the next is actually an expression of God's mercy. Because one generation did not overcome certain sins, they contend, full judgment would be deferred, and the next generation would have a chance to repent and escape God's full judgment for those sins.

In support of this concept, both First and Second Kings illustrate that the kingdoms of Israel and Judah were spared only a certain number of generations before God fully judged and destroyed them (see especially 2 Kings 17:7-23, 21:10-16 and 25:2-5).

Confession + Repentance

The Old Testament model of receiving forgiveness for sins includes confession of one's sins with the intention of repenting of, or turning away from, them:

Whoever confesses and forsakes then [sins] will have mercy. Proverbs 28:13, NKJ

This kind of confession, of both personal and corporate sin, was practiced throughout Israel's history. For example:

We lie down in our shame, and our confusion covereth us: for we have sinned against the LORD *our God, we and our fathers, from our youth even unto this day, and have not obeyed the voice of the* LORD *our God.*
Jeremiah 3:25

The people of Israel acknowledged the shame and reproach they had brought upon themselves. They had sinned against God since the days of their youth in the wilderness. Another example is found in the Psalms:

We have sinned with our fathers, we have committed iniquity, we have done wickedly. Psalm 106:6

This type of confession of sin is community wide, the connection of the present generation to the sins of the fathers.

Another example of this practice is seen in Daniel:

O Lord, to us belongeth confusion of face, to our kings, to our princes, and to our fathers, because we have sinned against thee.
And whiles I was speaking, and praying, and confess-

ing my sin and the sin of my people Israel, and presenting my supplication before the LORD my God for the holy mountain of my God.

Daniel 9:8 and 20

Corporate confession was not strictly an Old Testament phenomenon. It is also found in the history and teachings of the New Testament!

This type of corporate confession was also practiced by Ezra (see Ezra 9:6-15) and Nehemiah (see Nehemiah 1:6-7).

NEW TESTAMENT EXAMPLES

Corporate confession was not strictly an Old Testament phenomenon. It is also found in the history and teachings of the New Testament. Jesus, Peter and Paul all assumed and made passing mention of generational sin as an ongoing reality in their day (see Matthew 23:32-35, 1 Thessalonians and 1 Peter 1:18-19).

Many claim that John 9:3, where Jesus stated that a blind man's lack of sight had not been caused by either his own sin or his parent's sin, signaled an end to the Old Testament principle of generational sin. But Jesus was merely asserting that, in this particular case, generational sin and/or personal sin were not the cause of the blindness.

Others claim that corporate, or generational, sin is part of the Old Testament *"curse of the law"* mentioned in Galatians 3:13, from which Christ redeemed us. But as both Old Testament and New Testament scholars point out, the *"curse of the law,"* in this passage, is referring specifically to the covenant curse of Leviticus 26 and Deuteronomy 28.

The plural pronouns used in 1 John 1:9 (*"If we confess our sins"*) and in James 5:16 (*"Confess your faults one to another"*), clearly indicate the notion of corporate confession. The Scriptures clearly teach that God's people can seek and receive His forgiveness on a corporate level, for the sins of others, and this will lead to them releasing His grace for them to repent individually.

MOSES AND IDENTIFICATION REPENTANCE

Moses repented for all Israel, after their sin with the golden calf (see Exodus 32:9-14). Later, he again identified himself with sins he had not personally committed:

Pardon our iniquity and our sin. Exodus 34:9

The Lord replied to a similar prayer from Moses:

I have pardoned according to thy word.
Numbers 14:20

Moses' dramatic recitation led to God's pardon of the rebels.

Ezra and Identification Repentance

Ezra's identification repentance on behalf of the fifth century B.C. Jewish community of Jerusalem is seen in Ezra 9:6-15. Ezra felt an overwhelming sense of shame for the sin that had been committed, and his prayer was one of confession. Though he had not participated in this sin himself, he nevertheless identified with it.

In Ezra 9:7, Ezra further acknowledged that the people's sinful actions were part of their history. The whole nation—kings and priests, as well as the people—had sinned in the past, and they had suffered for it at the hand of the enemy kings in the surrounding lands. This suffering had included loss of life (the sword), loss of freedom (captivity), loss of property (plunder) and loss of honor (humiliation).

They were not without hope:

> *And now for a little space grace hath been showed from the LORD our God, to leave us a remnant to escape, and to give us a nail in his holy place, that our God may lighten our eyes, and give us a little reviving in our bondage. For we were bondmen; yet our God hath not forsaken us in our bondage, but hath extended mercy unto us in the sight of the kings of Persia, to give us a reviving,, to set up the house of our God, and to repair the desolations thereof, and to give us a wall in Judah and in Jerusalem.* Ezra 9:8-9

This phrase, *"a nail in his holy place,"* is a metaphor referring to a peg in the wall on which a utensil was hung. God's mercy had permitted the remnant of Israel to be fixed in the place God had chosen for them.

Ezra continued:

> *And now, O our God, what shall we say after this? for we have forsaken thy commandments, which thou hast commanded by thy servants the prophets, saying, The land, unto which ye go to possess it, is an unclean land with the filthiness of the people of the lands, with their abominations, which have filled it from one end to another with their uncleanness.*
>
> Ezra 9:10-11

Ezra confessed the sins of the nation by referring to what the prophets had preached:

> *And after all that is come upon us for our evil deeds, and for our great trespass, seeing that thou our God hast punished us less than our iniquities deserve, and hast given us such deliverance as this; Should we again break thy commandments, and join in affinity with the people of these abominations? wouldest not thou be angry with us till thou hadst consumed us, so that there should be no remnant nor escaping?*
>
> Ezra 9:13-14

Ezra ended his prayer, not by asking for forgiveness, but by declaring that God was righteous. The people of Israel were guilty and deserved whatever justice God chose to give them. God would have been just in consuming them, even to the point that there was no remnant or survivor. Ezra knew that God would show mercy.

Daniel's Breakthrough

This entire passage is thematically associated with the prayer of Daniel 10 and, therefore, with the angelic breakthrough described in the latter part of that chapter. Daniel was praying because he wanted to understand the vision God had given him. This suggests that identification repentance helps break through the efforts of satanic powers sent to keep people cut off from God and also enables God's people to receive fresh grace from His throne.

In Daniel 10:13, the prince of the kingdom of Persia who is mentioned cannot be a human ruler, for the conflict referred to here is in the spiritual, heavenly realm, as the allusion to Michael makes clear. The prince, therefore, must be understood as a satanic figure who was to supervise the affairs of Persia, inspiring its religious, social and political structures to works of evil. In his writings, Paul refers to *"principalities, powers, rulers of the darkness of this world, and spiritual wickedness in high places"* (Ephesians 6:12). These were demon spirits that had to be dealt with. Daniel was successful in receiving his breakthrough.

Occasional Sin Versus a Lifestyle of Sin

The sin described in 1 John 3:4-9 is not occasional sin,

but a consistent lifestyle of sin. If Christ was sinless and the purpose of His coming was to remove sin, then whoever abides in Him does not sin. Habitually sinful conduct, therefore, indicates an absence of fellowship with Christ. Thus, if we claim to be a Christian, but sin is our way of life, our status as children of God can legitimately be questioned. True believers practice righteousness, because the One in whom they dwell is righteous. Therefore, God's righteousness is revealed in His children through their conduct. Righteous conduct does not produce righteous character, but it does reveal its presence in us.

If Christ was sinless and the purpose of His coming was to remove sin, then whoever abides in Him does not sin!

In the same way, Satan's sinful nature is shown through the lives of those who belong to him. Jesus' announced purpose in coming to Earth was to destroy the devil's works (see 1 John 3:8). A person who sins, even a believer, is motivated by the devil (see 1 John 2:19). Thus, John is indicating that it is possible for believers to do that which is of the devil (see also Mark 8:31 and James 3:6).

The seed that remains in them is probably the divine nature, in which believers can participate (see 2 Peter 1:4), but the seed has been contaminated. In other words, this verse is saying that habitual sin is inconsistent with the Christian walk and must be dealt with. This is done through repentance, both individual and corporate. Learn to use this powerful tool.

The Violent Take It By Force. Will you be one of them?

Chapter 9

Mapping the Spirit World

Professing themselves to be wise, they became fools, and changed the glory of the uncorruptible God into an image made like to corruptible man, and to birds, and fourfooted beasts, and creeping things. Wherefore God also gave them up to uncleanness through the lusts of their own hearts, to dishonour their own bodies between themselves: who changed the truth of God into a lie, and worshipped and served the creature more than the Creator, who is blessed for ever. Amen.

Romans 1:22-25

Spiritual mapping is a means by which we can see what is beneath the surface of the material world!

Spiritual mapping is a means by which we can see what is beneath the surface of the material world. It is not confined to the works of darkness only. God also operates in the spiritual dimension, and we also want to see what He is doing.

Identifying the Redemptive Purpose

A crucial part of any spiritual mapping is to identify the redemptive purpose of a city or a nation. The redemptive purpose is the purpose that God had in His heart for that place. And this is not only important for a city or a nation, but also for individuals—you included. The goal of doing spiritual mapping is not just to expose satanic strongholds, unmask occultic deception or bind principalities and powers. The goal is to restore God's glory to every detail of His creation.

Knowing God's redemptive purposes provides specific and positive direction to our praying and other activities conducted for the purpose of doing spiritual warfare. Spiritual mapping is superimposing our understanding of forces and events in the spiritual domain onto places and circumstances in the material world.

The problem seems to be that many believers have not taken the time to learn the language, principles and protocols of spiritual dimensions. Spiritual mapping gives us the means to see what is beneath the surface of the material world. Such mapping is objective, in that it can be verified or discredited by history, sociological observation and God's Word.

In Daniel 10, for instance, we have a well-defined case of an evil spiritual being ruling over an entire area with explicitly prescribed boundaries. When this passage is studied with passages such as Ezekiel 28:12-19 and Deuteronomy 32:8 (*"according to the number of the angels of God,"* Septuagint) and Ephesians 6:12 (the word for *"world rulers"* is *kosmokratoras* in Greek), the case for spiritual territoriality becomes even more compelling.

How Territorial Strongholds Are Established

Let us look for a moment at how territorial strongholds are established. The Babel of Genesis 11 was a place in ancient Mesopotamia where people lived and were sent out by God into the four corners of the earth. Although little is known about the original movements of the first people groups out from Mesopotamia, what we do know suggests at least one experiential common denominator—trauma.

As the people spread out from Mesopotamia, all of them experienced trauma in one form or another. For some, it was the inability or difficulty of traveling because of mountain ramparts that blocked their path. For others, it was a sudden lack of sustenance, brought about by severe climatic conditions. Still others found themselves engaged in mortal combat with enemies along the way.

Whatever these ancient traumas might have been, they always had the effect of bringing people face to face with their desperation. How would they resolve their challenges? Each circumstance was an opportunity for a specific people in a specific place to return to God in repentance, thereby establishing Him as their rightful Ruler and sole Deliverer.

Sadly, the overwhelming majority of people, down through history, have elected to exchange the revelations of God for a lie. Heeding the entreaties of demons, they have chosen, in their desperation, to enter into pacts with the spirit world. In return for a particular deity's consent to resolve their immediate trauma, they offered up their singular and ongoing allegiance.

It is through the placement of these ancient welcome mats, or contracts, that demonic territorial strongholds were established. The transactions were entirely conscious. People made a choice to suppress truth and, instead, to believe a falsehood. That always opens a door to Satan.

Is this not what Paul addressed when writing to the Romans:

> *For the wrath of God is revealed from heaven against all ungodliness and unrighteousness of men, who hold the truth in unrighteousness; because that which may be known of God is manifest in them; for God hath showed it unto them. For the invisible things of him from the creation of the world are clearly seen, being understood by the things that are made, even his eternal power and Godhead; so that they are without excuse: because that, when they knew God, they glorified him not as God, neither were thankful; but became vain in their imaginations, and their foolish heart was darkened. Professing themselves to be wise, they became fools, and changed the glory of the uncorruptible God into an image made like to corruptible man, and to birds, and fourfooted beasts, and creeping things. Wherefore God also gave them up to uncleanness through the lusts of their own hearts, to dishonour their own bodies between themselves: who changed the truth*

of God into a lie, and worshipped and served the creature more than the Creator, who is blessed for ever. Amen. Romans 1:18-25

No wonder God's wrath results!

How Such Strongholds Are Maintained

The interesting thing is that such strongholds are often maintained from generation to generation. It is clear that earlier generations allowed demonic forces into certain neighborhoods, but how do these evil powers maintain their tenancy rights across centuries? One major answer to this question is found in the authority transfers that occur during religious festivals, ceremonies and pilgrimages. Spiritual power is released during these activities and has been testified to by numerous national believers and missionaries.

Religious festivals, ceremonies and pilgrimages are taking place somewhere in the world every week of the year. Literally thousands of these events take place, ranging from localized celebrations to regional and international affairs. Carnival, Halloween and the Islamic Haj are well recognized international examples; lesser known regional festivals such as Kumbha Mela in India, Inti Raymi in Peru and summer Bon celebrations in Japan, attract huge numbers of participants as well.

In this way, ancient contracts are constantly being renewed. These celebrations are decidedly not the benign, quaint and colorful cultural spectacles they are often made out to be. They are conscious transactions with the spirit world. They are opportunities for contemporary generations to reaffirm the choices and pacts made by their forefathers and ancestors. They are occasions to dust off ancient welcome mats and strengthen contracts with the spirit world.

> ***These celebrations are decidedly not the benign, quaint and colorful cultural spectacles they are often made out to be!***

At these affairs, legal rights are extended to the devil to rule over specific people and places, and so the significance of these events should never be underestimated. Hundreds of thousands of children a day are born into these enchanted systems around the world. Nearly all of them grow up hearing about a lie, but it is during the course of puberty rites and initiation that many of them feel its intense gravitational suction for the first item. The power of the lie, fueled by demonic magic, is called "tradition." It is tradition that sustains territorial dynasties.

WHERE SPIRITUAL MAPPING COMES IN

The enemy can be defeated with the help of spiritual mapping. The natural is only a reflection of the spiritual, and connection between them always exists. Isaiah 45:1-3 helps us realize that God reveals new information to His people so that we can perform better in battle and gain the victory. If God would go before Cyrus, *"His anointed,"* He will do the same for us today. He will prepare the way for us (see verse 2) and give us the treasures of darkness and the hidden riches of secret places (see verse 3).

In Ezekiel 4, the man of God was instructed (in verse 1): *"take thee a tile, and lay it before thee, and portray upon it the city, even Jerusalem."* God was instructing him to draw a layout of the city. In the following verses, he elaborates (verse 2), *"lay siege against it [the city], and build a fort against it, and cast a mount against it; set the camp also against it, and set battering rams against it round about."* When we take time to consider the community we are dealing with, we get an image of spiritual situations in the heavens.

Spiritual mapping gives us an image of the spiritual, a photograph, if you will, of the situation in the heavenly places above us. What an X-ray is to a physician, spiritual mapping is to intercessors. It is a supernatural vision that shows us the enemy's lines, location, number, weapons, and above all, how this enemy can be defeated.

The Role of Angels

There are millions of angels whom God has sent forth to minister to those who inherit salvation (see Hebrews 1:14), and these angels strictly obey His call. They are heavenly warriors who, as a disciplined army, receive their orders from Heaven itself. They come to our aid and help defeat the enemy (see Daniel 10:13, Psalm 19:11 and Revelation 12:7). Never underestimate the importance of the work of angels.

Specific Places of Importance

In the Old Testament, there is much mention of specific places, such as *" your high places"* (Leviticus 26:30), locations on high mountains or specific hills or certain trees, places which pagan nations had marked as the abode of specific gods or spirits (see Deuteronomy 12:2). God gave specific instruction to the Israelites that when they possessed these places for a place to live, they must first destroy all memory of the former gods, casting out their names and their spirits from those places.

The different nations all possessed specific gods and evil spirits which had specific names, such as Baal, Asherahs (see Judges 3:7) and Ashtaroths (see 1 Samuel 7:3-4). In Second Kings, we read:

> *Howbeit every nation made gods of their own, and put them in the houses of the high places which the Samaritans had made, every nation in their cities wherein they dwelt. And the men of Babylon made Succothbenoth, and the men of Cuth made Nergal, and the men of Hamath made Ashima, and the Avites made Nibhaz and Tartak, and the Sepharvites burnt their children in fire to Adrammelech and Anammelech, the gods of Sepharvaim.* 2 Kings 17:29-31

A very interesting observation on the power of territorial spirits is made in 1 Kings 20:23, where the officials of the king of Aram advised him: *"Their gods are gods of the hills. That is why they were too strong for us. But if we fight them on the plains, surely we will be stronger than they."* This expresses a clear belief, at least among those particular people, that spirits and gods had power only over certain limited areas of jurisdiction.

> ***In the story of Paul's extraordinary work in Ephesus, Acts 19 suggests that territorial spirits might have been at work!***

NEW TESTAMENT EXAMPLES

The examples of territorial spirits in the New Testament are limited. While there are many cases where demons and evil spirits are openly confronted, there are but a few times when the idea of those demons being attached to specific territories is recognized.

When Jesus was about to cast the demons from the possessed man in Mark 5:1-20, the demons begged Him not to send them out of that area. It would appear quite clear that the legion of demons belonged to that area and did not want to leave it. When the spirits were cast into the pigs and they ran into the lake and drowned, the people of that region seemed to be blinded by the power of those demons, for they were immediately afraid and began to plead for Jesus to leave their region (see verse 17).

In the story of Paul's extraordinary work in Ephesus, Acts 19 suggests that territorial spirits might have been at work. After Paul's open warfare with evil spirits (see verse 12), we read the account of the seven Jewish exorcists who were overpowered and beaten by the evil spirits in a man. However, this powerful encounter in the name of Jesus brought many to openly denounce Artemis, who appears to have been a principality over the evil spirits of that area around Ephesus.

So, there is enough evidence in the New Testament to convince us that we need to look beyond the mere appearance of things and know what power is at work behind them.

FOLLOWING BIBLICAL PRINCIPLES AND METHODS IN MAPPING

As with everything else we do for God, there are biblical principles that must guide our work. With spiritual mapping, we must, at the very least, be aware of the following:

- We must always base our ministry on God's Word and His revelation.
- We must be certain we are living in holiness before we go forth to attempt such a work.

- We must be sent by God in His time and with His authority.
- We must conduct our research according to the instructions we have received from Him.
- We must report our information without personal or prejudicial opinion.
- We must keep an attitude of faith in the power of God to make the necessary changes.

Various Levels of Spiritual Mapping

There are many levels of spiritual mapping. Mapping could be done in your neighborhood or in your particular section of a city. Mapping could be done for the city as a whole, for the city and its surrounding area, for the entire state or province, or for the entire nation. Here are some practical steps that can guide you:

Step One: Select a manageable geographical area with discernible spiritual boundaries.

Step Two: Gather the required information.

Your public library is a very good source for such information. Your courthouse might also provide legal records of the type of government over your city. Be sure to identify the personality of your city, area, etc.

Through historical research, discover any important information that is available. Once you get the information about the founder of the city, important events that took place in your city, what your city was known for and any other important facts, you can better determine the general purpose for which the city was founded. Spiritual forces shaping your city will be revealed as you discover the personality of the city through physical and spiritual research.

Step Three: Act on your acquired information.

Here are some practical things to do:

1. With pastors: Secure the unity of the pastors and other Christian leaders in the area and begin to pray together on a regular basis.

2. With the whole Body of Christ: Project a clear image that this effort is not an activity simply of Pentecostals or Charismatics, but of the whole Body of Christ. Get everyone working together.

Using practical steps like these, you can better understand spiritually the task set before you, and then, with the Lord's help, you can actually set out to accomplish it.

The Violent Take It By Force. Will you be one of them?

Part III

Confronting the Enemy

Chapter 10

Dealing with Iniquity

> *You shall not bow down to them nor serve them. For I, the LORD your God, am a jealous God, visiting the iniquity of the fathers upon the children to the third and fourth generations of those who hate Me.*
>
> Exodus 20:5, NKJ

Now that we know how important it is to confront the enemy and we know what tools we can use against him, we must discover some specific practices we can apply to defeat him. I want to discuss three in particular: dealing with iniquity, dealing with strongholds and redeeming the land.

The principle expressed in this verse is clear: God is a jealous God, and He will *"visit the iniquities"* of fathers upon children *"to the third and fourth generation."* What does that mean to us today? It is a truth noted in other passages, so it bears further examination.

> *You shall not bow down to them nor serve them. For I, the LORD your God, am a jealous God, visiting the iniquity of the fathers upon the children to the third and fourth generations of those who hate Me.*
>
> Deuteronomy 5:9, NKJ

> *In those days they shall say no more, The fathers have eaten a sour grape, and the children's teeth are set on edge.* Jeremiah 31:29

Let's see if we can understand this more fully.

THE DIFFERENCE BETWEEN SIN AND INIQUITY

We must begin with the truth that there is a significant difference between *sin* and *iniquity*. God said:

> *For I will be merciful to their unrighteousness, and their sins and their lawless deeds I will remember no more.*
>
> Hebrews 8:12, NKJ

For emphasis, this was repeated again later:

> *Their sins and their lawless deeds I will remember no more.*
>
> Hebrews 10:17, NKJ

Sin can be forgiven, and God no longer remembers it. Unless dealt with, however, the affects of iniquity continue from one generation to another.

God is a jealous God, and He will "visit the iniquities" of fathers upon children "to the third and fourth generation!"

WHAT THEN IS SIN AND WHAT IS INIQUITY?

The definition of *sin* is "to miss the mark" or "to break the law of God." *Iniquity*, on the other hand, means "to deviate from the proper path." David gives us some insight into this matter:

> *Behold, I was brought forth in iniquity, and in sin my mother conceived me.* Psalm 51:5, NKJ

We might say, then, that the difference between sin and iniquity is that sin is the cause, and iniquity is the effect. Sin is not passed down from one generation to another. Each of us will be judged for his or her own sins. Weakness to sin in a given area, however, is something altogether different. This is readily passed from father to child.

With sin, each individual has a choice either to give in or to resist. But each of us is plagued by learned and acquired behavioral patterns, and these are often set by one generation and followed by the next, the next and the next.

Because he was jealous of his brother, for instance, Cain became a murderer:

> *Now Cain talked with Abel his brother; and it came to pass, when they were in the field, that Cain rose up against Abel his brother and killed him.* Genesis 4:8, NKJ

Only Cain had to answer for this sin, but it is clear that the iniquity of it was passed on to his descendants:

> *Then Lamech said to his wives: "Adah and Zillah, hear my voice; wives of Lamech, listen to my speech! For I*

have killed a man for wounding me, even a young man for hurting me. Genesis 4:23, NKJ

Because Cain killed a man, his descendant Lamech was found to have a weakness for murder.

SPIRITUAL DEFORMITY CAUSED BY SIN

David's generational iniquity, mentioned in the psalms, stemmed from his ancestor Rahab and her life as a prostitute:

Behold, I was brought forth in iniquity, and in sin my mother conceived me. Psalm 51:5, NKJ

This power of iniquity was then passed on to Solomon. Such iniquities can affect entire cultures. Of Noah's generation, it was written:

This is the genealogy of Noah. Noah was a just man, perfect in his generations. Noah walked with God. Genesis 6:9, NKJ

There was, however, a weakness that was passed from Noah to his descendants:

Then he drank of the wine and was drunk, and became uncovered in his tent. And Ham, the father of Canaan, saw the nakedness of his father, and told his two brothers outside. Genesis 9:21-22, NKJ

Exposing the nakedness of a parent was forbidden by the Law:

> *None of you shall approach anyone who is near of kin to him, to uncover his nakedness: I am the LORD.*
>
> Leviticus 18:6, NKJ

The men of Sodom were aggressive homosexuals, bent on raping innocent travelers!

Ham disobeyed that law, and the consequences were serious:

> *So Noah awoke from his wine, and knew what his younger son had done to him. Then he said: cursed be Canaan; a servant of servants he shall be to his brethren.*
>
> Genesis 9:24-25, NKJ

Noah's other two sons, Shem and Japheth, took great pains to honor their father, not wanting even to glance at his nakedness. All three sons had been blessed because of their faithful father. When this happened, however, Noah cursed Ham indirectly, by cursing his son Canaan (see Genesis 9:25). The descendants of Canaan, the Canaanites, were in Sodom in Lot's day:

> *And they called to Lot and said to him, "Where are the men who came to you tonight? Bring them out to us that we may know them carnally."* Genesis 19:5, NKJ

The men of Sodom were aggressive homosexuals, bent on raping innocent travelers. Under the circumstance, Lot showed great courage by inviting his guests to stay at his house and there remain under his protection. The Hebrew verb here translated as *know* is ordinarily used in reference to normal heterosexual relations. Here, however, it is used to describe the perversion of homosexual sex, sex between men. This iniquity, or weakness toward sexual sin, was passed from generation to generation.

The Amorites worshipped false gods and the hosts of heaven. Of them, God said:

> *But in the fourth generation they shall return here, for the iniquity of the Amorites is not yet complete.*
>
> Genesis 15:16, NKJ

At the moment, the Lord was granting a stay of execution for the people of Canaan. He would wait to allow their sin to reach a critical level, and it would happen four generations later. In the interval, each succeeding generation increased in iniquity.

INIQUITY ALSO MEANS "GUILT"

The word *iniquity* also speaks of "guilt." The command of God to take the land from the Canaanite people would come only when their iniquity was *"complete."* But God had a remedy for their trouble. He said:

> *He shall see the labor of His soul, and be satisfied. By His knowledge My righteous Servant shall justify many, for He shall bear their iniquities. Therefore I will divide Him a portion with the great, and He shall divide the spoil with the strong, because He poured out His soul unto death, and He was numbered with the transgressors, and He bore the sin of many, and made intercession for the transgressors.* Isaiah 53:11-12, NKJ

Jesus became the all-time remedy for sin and iniquity. There is life in His blood:

> *For the life of the flesh is in the blood [nephesh], and I have given it to you upon the altar to make atonement for your souls; for it is the blood that makes atonement for the soul.* Leviticus 17:11, NKJ

Because of the blood of the Lamb that was slain before the foundation of the world, we can be free from all iniquity. We do not have to become as our ancestors. We can make a choice to accept the cleansing blood of Jesus and let it cleanse us from all sin and unrighteousness.

Righteousness Is Also Generational

Just as weaknesses can be transferred down through generations, blessings can also be transferred down through generations. When told that she would bring the Messiah into the world, Mary, the future mother of Jesus, responded:

> *For He has regarded the lowly state of His maidservant; for behold, henceforth all generations will call me blessed. For he who is mighty has done great things for me, and holy is His name. And His mercy is on those who fear Him from generation to generation.*
>
> Luke 1:48-50, NKJ

God's mercy expresses the Old Testament concept of God's loyal, gracious, faithful love extended to those who fear Him as a generation flowdown benefit.

Paul wrote to the Romans:

> *Nevertheless death reigned from Adam to Moses, even over those who had not sinned according to the likeness of the transgression of Adam, who is a type of Him who was to come.* Romans 5:14, NKJ

Timothy is an example of someone who received faith from his mother and grandmother:

> *When I call to remembrance the unfeigned faith that is in thee, which dwelt first in thy grandmother Lois, and thy mother Eunice; and I am persuaded that in thee also.* 2 Timothy 1:5

Timothy was blessed with *"unfeigned faith"* because he had a mother of unfeigned faith and a grandmother of unfeigned faith. Children nurtured in an environment of faith, hope and love learn to live in those spiritual elements. Their perspective on life is positive and encouraging because their faith has been built up and exercised through daily encounters with God. Consequently, any challenges they meet along the way are met with courage:

> *Even Levi, who receives tithes, paid tithes through Abraham, so to speak, for he was still in the loins of his father when Melchizedek met him.* Hebrews 7:9-10, NKJ

Levi was not yet born when Abraham paid tithes to Melchizedek, however, Levi was blessed and the windows of Heaven were opened over him because of the faithfulness of his ancestor in this regard.

So we see that there is such a thing as familial iniquity and familial blessing. Next, we must learn how to discover such family weaknesses and how to deal with them.

How to Determine and Deal with Family Iniquities

There are several things we can do to determine what iniquities might be troubling our family. For instance, we can look for ungodly patterns. Is there something that could be said of grandfather or mother that can also be said of children and/or grandchildren? Spirits attempt to oppress children as they have their forebears. Secondly, look for any iniquity that may have been passed down through familiar spirits.

Once you have recognized family iniquity, set about

to destroy it, once and for all. Doing that will require much perseverance on your part. There are varied methods that have been used. I can only tell you what has worked in my own life. Ask the Holy Spirit to guide you.

Fasting has always helped me. To understand the proper meaning of a fast, how to go about it and the results you should expect, study Isaiah 58.

Using the power of God's Word has also helped me. Meditate on that Word and make it your own. Then speak it with authority. It is one of the most effective tools we have against the enemy.

> *Is not My word like fire (that consumes all that cannot endure the test)? says the Lord, and like a hammer that breaks in pieces the rock (of most stubborn resistance)?*
>
> Jeremiah 23:29, AMP

There are several things we can do to determine what iniquities might be troubling our family!

The New King James Version promises this:

> *And they shall rebuild the old ruins, they shall raise up the former desolations, and they shall repair the ruined cities, the desolations of many generations.* Isaiah 61:4

Learn to discern and deal with iniquity, and you will be a successful intercessor, a blessing to all generations to come.

The Violent Take It By Force. Will you be one of them?

Chapter 11

Dealing with Strongholds

For though we walk in the flesh, we do not war after the flesh: (for the weapons of our warfare are not carnal [weapons of flesh and blood], *but mighty through God to the pulling down* [overthrow and destruction] *of strong holds;) casting down imaginations, and every high thing that exalteth itself against the knowledge of God, and bringing into captivity every thought to the obedience of Christ.*

2 Corinthians 10:3-5

A stronghold is "a forceful, stubborn argument, rationale, opinion, idea, and/or philosophy that is formed and resistant to the knowledge of Jesus Christ!"

What is a stronghold? It is "a forceful, stubborn argument, rationale, opinion, idea, and/or philosophy that is formed and resistant to the knowledge of Jesus Christ." The skillful use of spiritual weapons is required to break such a stronghold.

In the Amplified Bible, verse 5 states:

[Inasmuch as we] refute arguments and theories and reasonings and every proud and lofty thing that sets itself up against the [true] knowledge of God; and we lead every thought and pur-

pose away captive into the obedience of Christ (the Messiah, the Anointed One).

What Are Strongholds?

The Greek word translated *stronghold* is *ochuroma* and it means "to fortify through the idea of holding something safe." A stronghold is "what one uses to fortify and defend a personal belief, ideal or opinion against outside opposition." It is "the barricade around what you believe." It is set in place in defense of what you believe, especially when you are dead wrong.

Strongholds are like a thick, high wall, similar to the walls in the Middle Eastern cities of biblical days that were described as being as much as fifteen feet thick and twenty-five feet high. These dimensions give us some idea of the strength and all-encompassing power of a stronghold.

When a person is bound by a stronghold, they find protection and safety in that stronghold. The Canaanites lived behind such fortified walls. They didn't know, however, that the very walls they thought would protect them would actually become their destruction:

Now Jericho was straitly shut up because of the children of Israel: none went out, and none came in.

Joshua 6:1

This same thing can be said of a person who has erected a protective wall around their beliefs. Nothing is permitted in, and nothing is permitted out. You can give them truth, show them love, kindness and compassion, give them warnings, admonitions, exhortations or threats, and still they won't let any of it in. They are protected by a self-imposed wall surrounding what they believe.

Their wall is built to protect what *they* think is right, and they are committed to protecting and defending what they believe, at any cost, with active or passive resistance. They can sometimes be hostile or friendly in their defenses, but they are *"shut up"* or closed, to the truth, to deliverance, to help and even to impending judgment.

Anyone who threatens the safety of their stronghold is an enemy, and they will fight off all who challenge their spiritual and psychological status quo. Anything that doesn't line up with their perverted view is to be resisted at all costs. Anyone who attacks their belief becomes an enemy.

A stronghold also has the connotation of a castle. Every castle has a king ruling over it. The stronghold itself and the king over the stronghold are differentiated from each other.

The stronghold must be destroyed, and the king of that stronghold must also be defeated. If the stronghold is brought down but the king over it is not brought down, then that ruler will simply relocate, rebuild and continue his reign.

Jesus Himself said:

Or else how can one enter into a strong man's house, and spoil his goods, except he first bind the strong man? And then he will spoil his house. Matthew 12:29

When men and women have erected strongholds, new ideas cannot enter in and false ideas that are being protected cannot find their way out until you first bind the strongman that safeguards and maintains that belief. The king must be defeated before you can be free to accept right thoughts.

A good example of this is found in the book of Joshua:

And thou shalt do to Ai and her king as thou didst unto Jericho and her king. Joshua 8:2

When Joshua conquered Canaan in order to move the Israelites into the Promised Land, he had to overcome thirty-one different cities. He not only had to demolish those cities; he also had to capture and destroy the kings over them.

If Joshua, in his day, had to wage war against and overcome natural rulers, how much more do we have to defeat spiritual kings that set themselves up against our lives today? This is the reason Paul taught:

For we wrestle not against flesh and blood, but against principalities, against powers, against the rulers of the darkness of this world, against spiritual wickedness in high places. Ephesians 6:12

Our enemy is not natural, carnal or human; rather he is spiritual. When a family, a couple or a people hold on to opinions, behaviors, ideas and arguments that are contrary to the Word of God, they make themselves God's enemy. Strongholds can then be passed down from one generation to another as a legacy:

> ... *visiting the iniquity of the fathers upon the children unto the third and fourth generation of them that hate me.* Exodus 20:5

As we have noted, the blood of Jesus cleanses us from all unrighteousness and sets us free from generational curses, however families have a tendency to maintain weaknesses in the same area. Multigenerational dysfunctions have been observed throughout history. Some examples are co-dependency, marital conflict and substance abuse. It is not uncommon to find third- and fourth- generation patterns of divorce and abuse.

Strongholds have their own system to protect and defend themselves. They usually have an army of soldiers, regimented, armed and perched on the walls, ready to come to their defense. They will try to maim, kill and destroy anyone who tries to take their fortress.

Strongholds Differ from Person to Person

Strongholds differ from person to person, but there are notable common substructures. Perhaps the most common is fear. Fear can masquerade as hostility or aggressiveness. When King Saul threw a javelin at young David, fear was the root of his aggressive act.

Hostility is a cover-up for fear. Fear of closeness or intimacy can cause a husband to distance himself from his wife or vice versa. Sometimes people avoid the pain of another person leaving by avoiding relationships altogether.

The blood of Jesus cleanses us from all unrighteousness and sets us free from generational curses!

A second substructure is anger. When you touch a protected area, anger suddenly rises to the surface. Certain issues cannot be discussed in that person's presence, because they deny they are wrong and refuse to acknowledge your point. This anger may be either silent or warlike. Nevertheless anger is the force protecting the wrong idea, behavior, philosophy or opinion.

Destroying and overcoming strongholds is possible, but you cannot reason them out, wait for them to go away or pray them away. They will not automatically yield their positition with time. Strongholds are such resistant and formidable powers that only special weaponry can bring them down:

> *For the weapons of our warfare are not carnal, but mighty through God to the pulling down of strong holds.*
>
> 2 Corinthians 10:4

In actuality, we are all powerless against strongholds. Our only recourse is to use God's might to pull them down:

> *Above all, taking the shield of faith, wherewith ye shall be able to quench all the fiery darts of the wicked.*
>
> Ephesians 6:16

Satan's arsenal is mostly fiery darts, or projectiles, that are hurled at believers from a distance. The weapons at our disposal are superior to anything he can throw at us. Our weapons are mighty because they not only come from God, but they come through Him.

It is God's mighty power that is behind the weapons He has given us. His might is what makes them spiritually lethal.

Our spiritual weapons are also powerful because they are founded in the Word of God, and the Word instructs in their correct usage.

The Word of God itself is a weapon. It is the Spirit's sword. We may use it, but it is His. This is the reason it is the Holy Spirit who best qualifies us to use that Word.

The primary role of the Holy Spirit is to help believers to prepare for war. He is our military instructor:

> *Howbeit when he, the Spirit of truth, is come, he will guide you into all truth: for he shall not speak of himself; but whatsoever he shall hear, that shall he speak: and he will show you things to come.* John 16:13

The Mind Is the Battlefield

Our mind is a battlefield. The enemy uses thoughts to attack us. The process he uses is to introduce thoughts to our minds. Then those thoughts spread to outer areas of our lives, eventually affecting our whole life and the lives of everyone around us. And since strongholds are built in the mind, that's where the Word works to destroy them:

> *For the word of God is quick, and powerful, and sharper than any two-edged sword, piercing even to the dividing asunder of soul and spirit, and of the joints and marrow, and is a discerner of the thoughts and intents of the heart.* Hebrews 4:12

The Amplified Bible says this of the Sword of the Spirit:

> *For the Word that God speaks is alive and full of power [making it active, operative, energizing, and effective]; it is sharper than any two-edged sword, penetrating to the dividing line of the breath of life (soul) and [the immortal] spirit, and of joints and marrow [of the deepest parts of our nature], exposing and sifting and analyzing and judging the very thoughts and purposes of the heart.*

The Word of God is the only sword that can cut to the center of a person's psyche and pierce down to one's very soul, heart and thoughts.

> ***In ancient times, when wars were still fought with swords, men used those swords to kill the builders of the strongholds, not the structure of the strongholds themselves!***

How Swords Are to Be Used

In ancient times, when wars were still fought with swords, men used those swords to kill the builders of the strongholds, not the structure of the strongholds themselves. Swords were used on the people protecting the walls, not on the walls themselves. In the same way, the Word of God is to be used directly on Satan and his demons, for it is they who have established the strongholds in the first place.

Jesus used His Father's Word when He was led by the Spirit into the wilderness to be tempted of the devil:

> *But He answered and said, It is written, Man shall not live by bread alone, but by every word that proceedeth out of the mouth of God.* Matthew 4:4

When the Word is used, it defeats the century who guards the fortress. Learn to use yours well.

The Weapon of the Spirit Itself

Another equally powerful weapon to be used against strongholds is the Spirit of God:

> *Then he answered and spake unto me, saying, This is the word of the* Lord *unto Zerubbabel, saying, Not by might, nor by power, but by my Spirit, saith the* Lord *of hosts.* Zechariah 4:6

Think about it! The Holy Spirit Himself is a weapon. Because of this, He is often symbolized by fire. Historically, fire was used in two ways to destroy strongholds: It was used to burn down the standing wall, and to burn up the remains after a city had been besieged.

Burning up the dross in our lives is one of the works of the Holy Spirit today:

> *I will turn my hand upon thee, and purely purge away thy dross, and take away all thy tin.* Isaiah 1:25

He is still the Spirit of fire:

> *I indeed baptize you with water unto repentance: but he that cometh after me is mightier than I, whose shoes I am not worthy to bear: he shall baptize you with the Holy Ghost, and with fire.* Matthew 3:11

> *When the Lord shall have washed away the filth of the daughters of Zion, and shall have purged the blood of*

Jerusalem from the midst thereof by the spirit of judgment, and by the spirit of burning. Isaiah 4:4

Fire burns, consumes and destroys, and strongholds not only must be pulled down with the Word; they must also be burned by the fire of the Holy Spirit. Joshua knew this truth:

And they burnt the city with fire, and all that was therein: only the silver, and the gold, and the vessels of brass and of iron, they put into the treasury of the house of the LORD. Joshua 6:24

After the fall of the stronghold of Jericho, Joshua destroyed the city with fire. Ask the Holy Spirit to burn up any residue left in you after the Word has pulled down the walls in your life. And learn to use this same tactic in your intercessory ministry for others.

Satan Is Often Behind the Thoughts of Well-Meaning Christians

Often we fail to recognize that it is Satan who has planted a certain thought in us. Because of this, we must evaluate our every thought to make sure it lines up with the Word of God. If it doesn't, then reject it. You have that authority. God has said:

No weapon formed against you shall prosper.
Isaiah 54:17, NKJ

A thought from Satan is a weapon, and if you leave it unchallenged, it will surely do you harm. You are the one who has to condemn that tongue, condemn that thought. You are the one who must rebuke Satan and his lies. Don't ask God to do it. You do it. Jesus said:

> *Behold, I give unto you power to tread on serpents and scorpions, and over all the power of the enemy: and nothing shall by any means hurt you.* Luke 10:19

This is your authorization to rebuke Satan and his lies.

God expects you to reject every devilish thought. We are instructed to pull down every stronghold, cast down imaginations and every high thing and bring into captivity every thought to the obedience of Christ Jesus. If a thought comes to you that is contrary to the Word of God, therefore, you are to dismiss it.

WHY STRONGHOLDS WON'T LET GO

Strongholds are things that hold us tightly and won't let go. They are opinions that we allow to control us. So, in order to deal with strongholds, you must look at reality, and the greatest reality is God's Word.

The key lies not in finding where to place the blame, but in releasing the protective layers you have placed over your own pain so that God can make you whole. You can remove layers of self-defensive mechanisms you have placed over the unmet needs, unhealed hurts and unresolved issues of your past. You do this, again, by using God's Word:

> *And I will give unto thee the keys of the kingdom of heaven: whatsoever thou shalt bind on earth, shall be bound in heaven: and whatsoever thou shalt loose on earth shall be loosed in heaven.* Matthew 16:19

You must take authority by smashing, crushing, destroying, tearing apart and tearing down strongholds that have been built around these things. Only then can the healing grace and mercy of God flow freely into the wounded areas of vulnerability within your soul—your neediness, pain and confusion. Do the same for others.

It is important to remember that even though you don't see anything happening in the natural realm, God is moving mountains in the Spirit realm for you because you have chosen to align your will with His. Pray for the manifestation in the natural realm of what is being accomplished in the spiritual realm by the power of His Spirit.

The Erection of Strongholds

Our experiences play an important role in erecting strongholds. A mind filled with unresolved memories and unmet needs from the past is a mind clogged with pain, and it will cloud and pollute the truth it receives today.

Unmet needs and unresolved memories from the past

become the source of strongholds, protecting distorted ideas, attitudes and patterns of thinking today.

Strongholds may have enabled you to survive terrifying circumstances in your past that were out of your control. This is why you trust them. But if they are still in place in your life, they are providing access for the enemy's attack.

> ***You must take authority by smashing, crushing, destroying, tearing apart and tearing down strongholds that have been built around these things!***

We build the strongholds, we rely on them to protect us and we fight like crazy to keep them. We erect a stronghold around things we cannot bear to face. Strongholds and what they protect often cross and overlap the categories of wrong attitudes, patterns of thinking and beliefs. But, again, a stronghold is what we rely upon to defend and protect our right to believe something.

When we are painfully deceived we can build a stronghold of suspicion to protect against being deceived again. Rejection can cause you to build up a stronghold of independence and self-sufficiency around pain, fortifying a right to never be vulnerable again.

When someone has been abused or deeply hurt, unless forgiveness and healing comes, then strongholds of unforgiveness, bitterness or anger are erected to justify the role of being a victim. Betrayal can cause the building of a stronghold of distrust to prevent anyone from getting close enough to betray you again.

A childhood filled with chaos, instability and everything seemingly out of control can build a stronghold of control, to prevent ever being at the mercy of another again. A stronghold is built to justify and protect the right to indulge self, to compensate for unmet needs and pain. This stronghold also justifies a right to chemically alter reality with drugs or alcohol, to blot out pain.

Denial is a valid, temporary mental and emotional coping mechanism that enables the human mind to survive certain traumatic situations, very much like shock shuts down and prevents a severely wounded body from death. Denial enables abused children to survive unbearable situations. But just as shock becomes dangerous and life threatening when a person cannot come out of it, so does denial when it becomes a stronghold. Learn to recognize these strongholds and deal with them so that they don't rob you of your destiny.

You'll Know

How can you know you're dealing with a stronghold? You know when:

- A family member refuses to change their behavior, even though they know it would benefit them personally.

- A family member refuses to change their behavior even though they know it is destructive and injurious to their life, health or welfare.
- Marital and/or family problems have not changed over a period of time, and have even gotten worse, despite all human effort.
- Marriage partners or other family members are blinded to their own faults, but are able to see everyone else's.
- Family members cannot control human desires and impulses and have no desire to do so.
- A family member is consistently and openly hostile to the Gospel.

Be ready to fight for your loved one's deliverance.

The enemy hides in the mind, will, emotions, memories, experiences and beliefs. Wrong attitudes, wrong ideas, wrong behaviors and old mindsets can keep you and others from receiving the truth. Hear the words of David:

> *Let God arise, let his enemies be scattered: let them also that hate him flee before him.* Psalm 68:1

PAUL'S PERSPECTIVE

Overlooking ancient Corinth was a hill nearly two thousand feet high, and on top of that hill was a fortress. Paul used that imagery as an illustration of the spiritual warfare he waged. He destroyed strongholds, cast down

Paul cast down all rationalizations. He took captive to the obedience of Christ every perception and intention of the heart that was against God and God's will!

towers and took captives. The fortress, towers and captives represent the arguments, thoughts and plans that Paul was opposing. Paul cast down all rationalizations. He took captive to the obedience of Christ every perception and intention of the heart that was against God and God's will.

Our actions reveal our thoughts. Therefore we should not cling to thoughts that fail to conform to the life and the teachings of Christ. Paul did not walk according to the flesh or his worldly desires. Instead, he fought daily to conquer the flesh. He explained his strategy to the Corinthian believers:

Know ye not that they which run in a race run all, but one receiveth the prize? So run, that ye may obtain. And every man that striveth for the mastery is temperate in all things. Now they do it to obtain a corruptible crown; but we an incorruptible. I therefore so run, not as uncertainly; so fight I, not as one that beateth the air: but I keep under my body, and bring it into

subjection: lest that by any means, when I have preached to others, I myself should be a castaway.
1 Corinthians 9:24-27

Bondage begins in the mind, but freedom also begins in the mind. Therefore, it pays to guard your mind.

Keep thy heart with all diligence; for out of it are the issues of life. Proverbs 4:23

Thoughts can captivate your mind, hold your life in a vice and keep you from the truth. How long will they hold you? Just as long as you permit them to.

When a man named Simon offered Paul money to receive his power, Paul advised him:

Repent therefore of this thy wickedness, and pray God, if perhaps the thought of thine heart may be forgiven thee. Acts 8:22

Simon was said to be a believer, but he had somehow confused the work of God with his previous magical practices. Others paid him for the secrets of his magic, so he may have thought that this was the best way to approach receiving the gift of God. The point is that what you think gets into your heart and affects it. Jesus Himself said:

For out of the heart proceed evil thoughts, murders, adulteries, fornications, thefts, false witness, blasphe-

mies: these are the things which defile a man: but to eat with unwashen hands defileth not a man.

Matthew 15:19-20

The Scriptures sums it all up like this:

For as he thinketh in his heart, so is he. Proverbs 23:7

Wow! You are what you think. Thoughts get into the heart, which is the seat of reflection, and they come through the eye gate, the ear gate and the other senses. So what we allow into our mind makes its way to our heart, and that determines who and what we are. So what we think affects our way of life, our attitude toward life and ultimately our interaction with others. So learn to recognize and deal with strongholds, and you will not only find deliverance for yourself, but also become an effective intercessor for others.

The Violent Take It By Force. Will you be one of them?

Chapter 12

Redeeming the Land

And God spake all these words, saying, I am the LORD thy God, which have brought thee out of the land of Egypt, out of the house of bondage. Thou shalt have no other gods before me. Exodus 20:1-3

Certain conditions or events give evil spirits a legal right to set up a base of operation in our lives. In this chapter, we will discuss a few of these. Ruling spirits have no authority to move into an area without permission to do so. Certain conditions give them authority to set up the base of their kingdom, from which they can rule over the people in that area. Remove the favorable conditions, and you can remove the spirits and redeem the land.

Thou shalt not make unto thee any graven image, or any likeness of any thing that is in heaven above, or that is in the earth beneath, or that is in the water under the earth. Thou shalt not bow down thyself to them, nor serve them: for I the LORD thy God am a jealous God, visiting the iniquity of the fathers upon the children unto the third and fourth generation of them that hate me. Exodus 20:4-5

IDOLATRY

God clearly commanded Israel that they must never have anything at all to do with any graven image. This was because idols represent evil spirits (see 1 Corinthians 10:10-20). Often a demon spirit is attached to a particular idol because the idol, after it is made, has been dedicated to that spirit. Therefore, it is his idol, and he has a legal right to be anywhere that idol is. This is the reason the idol must not be stored or hidden away, smashed, thrown out, etc. Instead, it must be totally destroyed by fire (see Deuteronomy 7:5).

Often, a home will be contaminated by an idol that is kept there or worshipped there, and that home must be cleansed. Here are some practical steps to take:

Certain conditions or events give evil spirits a legal right to set up a base of operation in our lives!

1. Pray together and claim the protection of the blood of Jesus before beginning.
2. Sing a suitable hymn, such as "There Is Power in the Blood."
3. Read a suitable scripture, such as Joshua 24:15, *"But as for me and my house, we will serve the* LORD*"* or, perhaps, a more lengthy one, such as Exodus 20:1-5.
4. After that, in the name of Jesus, you can tear down the idols from their pedestals or places of preeminence.
5. Say something like this, "In the name of Jesus, I tear you down from your seat of authority and cast you from this household. Your spirit shall not rule over these people anymore."

6. Take the idols and all the emblems of worship connected with them outside, place them on a pile and burn them right there (if you can). In the case of a high-rise apartment or other place where it is impossible to burn the items, carry them off to be burned elsewhere.
7. Now invite the Lord and His angels to come into the home to protect it and bless it.
8. Sing and praise the Lord, dedicating that home to Him. If possible, place some appropriate scriptural motto in the place of honor where the idol has once stood.

Some idols are worth fabulous amounts of money, but they should never be sold. God has said that they should be destroyed, and this is because if they are not destroyed, the demonic ruling spirit to which they are dedicated will accompany them to the next place, bringing with them their evil powers and gaining a legal foothold in that new area.

Clear instructions for how to deal with idols can be found in the book of Deuteronomy:

> *The graven images of their gods shall ye burn with fire: thou shalt not desire the silver or gold that is on them, nor take it unto thee, lest thou be snared therein: for it is an abomination to the* Lord *thy God. Neither shalt thou bring an abomination into thine house, lest thou be a cursed thing like it: but thou shalt utterly detest it, and thou shalt utterly abhor it; for it is a cursed thing.* Deuteronomy 7:25-26

TEMPLES TO PAGAN RELIGIONS

We have been critical of King Solomon and other Israelite kings who built high places, temples of a sort, to foreign gods, yet we have done the same thing in our own nations. The Hindus build their temples and erect their gods here in our country, and instead of working against them, we make these sites a tourist attraction. We have either forgotten or we have no understanding of the fact that, by doing this, we are giving the demon spirits a legal base from which to operate.

This has brought a curse upon our land. As our land is gradually given over to those coming in who serve other gods, there has come a surge of evil of every kind, such as extreme indulgence in sensuality, incest, illegal drugs, the worship of devils and a terrible scourge of witchcraft and Boba. God told Israel that they were responsible to enforce the laws of righteousness that He had given them and to make sure that the foreigner who chose to dwell in their land kept those same laws (see Leviticus 18:26).

MURDER, THE SHEDDING OF INNOCENT BLOOD

Thou shalt not kill. Exodus 20:13

Murder brings with it a curse. When Cain killed his brother Abel, God said:

And now art thou cursed from the earth, which hath opened her mouth to receive thy brother's blood from thy hand. Genesis 4:11

Murder is "the shedding of innocent blood in a violent way." Shedding innocent blood does not mean that the blood needs to be poured out. Any kind of murder is evil and brings a curse.

When we murder, or kill, someone, we are killing an extension of God, for man is made in the image of God!

After the flood, God told Noah:

Whoso sheddeth man's blood, by man shall his blood be shed: for in the image of God made he man.
Genesis 9:6

This law was reinforced through God's later command to Moses, and the reason God said it was that the life is in the blood:

For the life of the flesh is in the blood. Leviticus 17:11

When we murder, or kill, someone, we are killing an extension of God, for man is made in the image of God. The only way this great crime can be atoned for is by the murderer himself giving his life in payment for the one he has killed. That was Old Testament law.

Today, Jesus has died for all men's transgressions and

sins, including the sin of murder. If anyone accepts the shed blood of Jesus in payment for his own crime of murder, that one can go free of judgment. That is the only condition under which a person can escape great punishment. He has to acknowledge that Jesus suffered in his place. The law is *"a life for a life"* (Deuteronomy 19:21). In this case, it's either the life of Christ or the life of the murderer.

Murder brings a curse, not only on the doer, but also on the place where the murder has been committed. Satan wants to bring God's curse on people and nations and their land, and he knows that the shedding of innocent blood will work quickly to turn the favor of God away from us. For this reason, Satan uses wars, riots, rebellion, the sacrifice of humans in satanic rites and anger, which results in murder. Satan's masterstroke of genius showed itself right here in the United States of America, when the Supreme Court of our land made a ruling making abortion prior to the last ten weeks of pregnancy a legal option. In doing this, men overruled the laws of God.

In the process, this country has brought a curse upon itself like no nation in history. And if shedding innocent blood brings a curse, then our doctors, nurses and midwives who commit this crime every day are cursed. Our hospitals and clinics where abortions take place are cursed. The Supreme Court that condoned this brutal act is cursed. The wombs of those who became the case area where the crime took place are cursed. And anyone who helps and cooperates with this evil is cursed.

When innocent blood is shed, we give Satan a legal

right over our nation, our cities, our government and our individual lives. His spirits of murder have been unleashed to destroy any life he wishes to extinguish. Satan has caused murder to become so commonplace that today, because of our laws against capital punishment in many states, murderers are allowed to live, even though God has plainly said: *"the murderer shall surely be put to death"* (Numbers 35:17).

Murder pollutes the land, and only the death of the slayer redeems the land from the curse:

> *So ye shall not pollute the land wherein ye are: for blood it defileth the land: and the land cannot be cleansed of the blood that is shed therein, but by the blood of him that shed it.* Numbers 35:33

Witchcraft, Covens and Obea

Satanism and witchcraft are multiplying across our land at a dramatic rate. Even the well educated are now enticed into this deceit by their desire to delve into the unknown. In Great Britain alone, an estimated forty thousand people are involved in witchcraft and magic. Covens are being established throughout our Western nations. And wherever there is a witches' coven, the spirits have a legal right to invade that territory.

Thus, every center of witchcraft is a base for satanic operation. At first, Satan only demands the blood sacrifice of animals (such as dogs, cats and domesticated beasts of the field), but as soon as he gets firm control, he begins to demand human sacrifices—preferably innocent children. With the slaughter of every child, the spirits gain a legal stronghold over that area (see Leviticus 20:6).

THE REMOVAL OF PRAYER FROM OUR PUBLIC SCHOOLS

The children of Israel were taught the Word of God (see Exodus 12:26-28 and Deuteronomy 4:9 and 6:7). When children have prayer in their classrooms, there is a special spiritual covering and protection over them. If prayer is taken out of schools, our educational system becomes a vacuum for spirits to fill with their evil substitutes.

Instead of prayer, our children are now subjected to such things as transcendental meditation, yoga, pagan religions, misguided and immorally-taught sex education (which encourages sodomy and masturbation in the name of "alternative life-styles" and promotes promiscuity, resulting in teenage pregnancies, with the accompanying consequences of abortion and other tragedies).

Witchcraft, satanism and magic are all now part of our educational curriculum, and, as a result, crime is increasing in our schools to such a degree that in some larger cities police officers must be assigned to permanently patrol school hallways and playgrounds.

A substitute for the Word of God is humanism. Humanism is Satan's sugarcoated poisonous pill of rebellion against all good traditions and teachings. As Paul Kurts, Professor Emeritus of Philosophy at the State University of New York at Buffalo and confirmed humanist, said, "Secular humanists are committed to the use of reason and science to understand the world and solve social problems without 'the illusion of salvation or morality.' "

When we assume God's position and take it upon ourselves to solve problems which only deity can handle, we make ourselves out to be gods. The worship of self is dangerously evil.

Adultery, Sodomy, Perversion and Other Sex Sins

There must have been some sound and reasonable purpose that God commanded adulterers to be put to death in Old Testament times:

> *And the man that committeth adultery with another man's wife, even he that committeth adultery with his neighbour's wife, the adulterer and the adulteress shall surely be put to death.* Leviticus 20:10

Adultery causes anger, deep, deep grief and terrible heartache. It wears down the moral strength of man, church and nation. Ninety percent of the time adultery is caused by the demon spirit of lust. Therefore, it gives the demon spirit a legal base from which to operate.

Sodomy is a sin that brings with it a curse:

> *Thou shalt not lie with mankind, as with womankind: it is abomination.* Leviticus 18:22

A spirit of perversion comes with this sin. Behind it is

the sin of rebellion, disrespect and perversion. The spirits that are related to this type of activity are unclean, and they cause the breakdown of normal family life.

God says that those who commit the sin of sodomy are given over *"to uncleanness"*:

> *Wherefore God also gave them up to uncleanness through the lusts of their own hearts, to dishonour their own bodies between themselves: who changed the truth of God into a lie, and worshipped and served the creature more than the Creator, who is blessed for ever. Amen. For this cause God gave them up unto vile affections: for even their women did change the natural use into that which is against nature: and likewise also the men, leaving the natural use of the woman, burned in their lust one toward another; men with men working that which is unseemly, and receiving in themselves that recompense of their error which was meet. And even as they did not like to retain God in*

When we assume God's position and take it upon ourselves to solve problems which only deity can handle, we make ourselves out to be gods!

their knowledge, God gave them over to a reprobate mind, to do those things which are not convenient.
Romans 1:24-28

Sodomists and prostitutes are identical twins. They both sell or rent their organs of reproduction to satisfy perverted spirits of lust. Again, God said:

Thou shalt not lie with mankind, as with womankind: it is abomination. Leviticus 18:22

If a man also lie with mankind, as he lieth with a woman, both of them have committed an abomination: they shall surely be put to death; their blood shall be upon them. Leviticus 20:13

This word *abomination* is translated from the Hebrew *towebah,* and means "something which is morally disgusting." It comes from the root word *taab,* "to loath, detest, to morally abhor."

Sodomy and prostitution have historically both been connected with pagan temple rites. Both received official sanction from the religious leaders of the Canaanites. During the Kali Festival in India still today, there are seasons of sexual orgy associated with Astarte.

Incest and Bestiality

Sexual intercourse with a family member is called incest, and Leviticus 18 and 20 warn strictly against this sin and decree the death sentence as the proper punishment for it. Nothing more need be said.

Bestiality, more common than is known or recognized, unleashes dreadful plagues that can destroy a nation. It comes about because of a breakdown in the natural law of procreation that decrees that each should produce *"after his kind"* (Genesis 1:25). By breaking these high laws set by the Creator, we give the spirits of bestiality a legal right to possess us and have dominion over us.

ALCOHOLISM, HYPNOSIS AND THE USE OF DRUGS

All three of these work the same effects on a person's mind. They cause the person to enter a mental stage of illusion and unreality, in which they lose control of their inner moral strength. These sins cause people to do things they would not normally do.

I was struck by the testimony of Dr. George G. Ritchie, M. D., in his book, *Return from Tomorrow* (Old Tappan: Fleming Revell, 1978). He witnessed the spirits' takeover and possession of a man who was intoxicated, and it explains why people who are drunk become violent and dangerous. The evil spirit has control of them. This also explains why, when a moral person drinks too much, he can easily be influenced to commit adultery or other sins against God and man. Under the influence of these substances, one can easily lose control and be persuaded to do things which one will later deeply regret.

Dr. Ritchie died and in his spirit body was allowed to visit a bar. (Jesus was accompanying him.) Inside that dingy place, he saw that living people were surrounded by a faint, luminous glow, like an electrical field, over the entire surface of their bodies. His own spirit-body did not have it. He wrote:

> At this point, the Light drew me inside a dingy bar and grill near what looked like a large naval base. A crowd of people, many of them sailors, lined the bar three deep, while others jammed wooden booths along the wall. Though a few were drinking beer, most of them seemed to be belting whiskies as fast as the two perspiring bartenders could pour them.

Living people were surrounded by a faint, luminous glow, like an electrical field, over the entire surface of their bodies!

Then Dr. Ritchie noticed a striking thing. A number of the men standing at the bar seemed unable to lift their drinks to their lips. Over and over he watched them clutch at their shot glasses, hands passing through the solid tumblers, through the heavy wooden countertop, through the very arms and bodies of the drinkers around them. And these men, every one of them, lacked the aureole of light that surrounded the others. He realized:

> The cocoon of light must be a property of physical bodies only. The dead, we who had lost our solidness, had lost this "second skin" as well. And it was obvious that these living people, the light-surrounded ones, the ones actually drinking, talking, jostling each other, could neither see the desperately thirsty, disembodied beings among them, nor feel their frantic pushing to get at those glasses. (Though it was also clear to me, watching, that the non-solid people could both see and hear each other. Furious quarrels were constantly breaking out among them over glasses that none could actually get to his lips.)

Dr. Ritchie watched one young sailor rise unsteadily from a stool, take two or three steps, and then sag heavily to the floor.

> Two of his buddies stooped down and started dragging him away from the crush … . I was staring in amazement as the bright cocoon around the unconscious sailor simply opened up. It parted at the very crown of his head and began peeling away from his head, his shoulders. Instantly, quicker than I had ever seen anyone move, one of the insubstantial beings who had been standing near him at the bar was on top of him. He had been hovering, like a thirsty shadow at the sailor's side, greedily following every swallow the young man made. Now he seemed to spring at him like a beast of prey. In

the next instant, to my utter mystification, the springing figure had vanished.

It all happened, even before the two men had dragged their unconscious body from under the feet of those at the bar. One minute I had distinctly seen two individuals; by the time they propped the sailor against the wall, there was only one. Twice more, as I stared, stupefied, the identical scene was repeated. A man passed out, a crack swiftly opened in the aureole around him, and one of the non-solid people vanished, as he hurled himself at the opening, almost as if he had scrambled inside the other man.

Was that covering of light some kind of shield then? Was it a protection against disembodied beings like myself? Presumably these substance-less creatures had once had solid bodies, as I myself had. I suppose that when they had been in these bodies they had developed a dependence on alcohol that went beyond the physical. That became mental. Spiritual, even. Then, when they lost that body, except when they could briefly take possession of another one, they would be cut off for all eternity from the thing they could never stop craving.

Heed the good doctor's warning.

Fighting, Anger, Quarrelsomeness, Hatred and an Unforgiving Spirit

Strong, negative emotions give Satan a legal right to a

person. A home where there is fighting and quarreling becomes an easy prey of the devil.

There are many Christian families who need to have their relationships corrected. We need to make peace, if possible, with those with whom we have had disagreements.

Never go to sleep without confessing your sins. Unconfessed sin, even in the heart of a Christian, can give the spirits a legal foothold. We must always *"examine ourselves"* (1 Corinthians 11:28).

When we are filled with unconfessed anger, Satan has every right to strike us with sickness or demon possession. The unconfessed and unrepented sins of the Christians give Satan a lot more authority over us than we could ever realize. If we could see the consequences of our pride and love of self, we would be filled with remorse and regret.

Objects Used in Connection with Black Magic, Witchcraft and Satan Worship

When an object is used in connection with the spirit world, it is dedicated to the devil. From that time on, his spirits are attached to that object. Temple idols, house gods, instruments used in connection with worship, such as crystal balls, ouija boards, tarot cards, some works of art and even buildings, have demonic connections. Learn to deal with all of these wisely and biblically.

Dirty Movies, Magazines and Music

There is no doubt that spirits of violence and lust accompany the conception and production of some music, theatrical performances, television programs, pornographic magazines, films and pornographic sites on the Internet. Photos of nudity and violence work on those who come to devour this type of "garbage." Be warned! You become what you eat—physically and spiritually!

Rock music, with its subliminal messages (hidden by its backward masking), has destroyed many lives. Much of that music has been dedicated to Satan. His evil spirits, therefore, have every right to accompany such recordings and their playback. Parents are responsible to supervise the music their children listen to and on which they spend their hard-earned money.

Unhealthy Relationships

The relationships we maintain with others have a very definite influence on us, either for good or for bad. The Word of God discourages God's people from making intimate alliances with the ungodly or those who would be a bad influence on us. This is to protect the healthy from being infected with any deadly or incurable disease (see Leviticus 13:5, 21, 33, 46 and Numbers 5:3).

Samson fell in love with a pagan woman named Delilah (see Judges 16:20-31), and she proved his undoing. Be advised that even though a man or woman may profess to be a Christian, and they may not have an evil heart, it could just take that person's moral weakness and their passion to make a union that will destroy the other forever.

Good biblical examples of this are Abraham and Hagar and David and Bathsheba. There was a man in the church at Corinth who had an unhealthy relationship with his father's wife (1 Corinthians 5:1). Paul was compelled to warn others about it.

Satan uses our passions and naivete to lead many into unholy relationships. Don't make yourself available for the devil to destroy your life in this way (and maybe even your soul).

We cannot emphasize too strongly the importance of marriage between those of like faith:

> *Be ye not unequally yoked together with unbelievers: for what fellowship hath righteousness with unrighteousness? and what communion hath light with darkness? And what concord hath Christ with Belial? or what part hath he that be-*

There is no doubt that spirits of violence and lust accompany the conception and production of some music, theatrical performances, television programs, pornographic magazines and films!

lieveth with an infidel? And what agreement hath the temple of God with idols? for ye are the temple of the living God; as God hath said, I will dwell in them, and walk in them; and I will be their God, and they shall be my people. 2 Corinthians 6:14-16

Inordinate Affection

Whenever the devotion between two people is greater than their love for God, Satan has a legal right to bind them together with such strong soul-ties that both will be blinded to truth and to purity. There can be unholy and unclean relationships between two people of the same sex, which will pull both persons down.

It is better for some people to be separated from each other because of the bad influence they have on each other. Some good biblical examples are Simeon and Levi (see Genesis 49:5-7).

A Picture of Satan's Strategy

The overall picture of Satan's strategy is something like this: he places a canopy over his triangle, under which his evil spirits can operate. This canopy establishes the perimeter of the area where the spirits are free to work unhindered. That is why certain sins are more prevalent over specific areas. Crime, murders, sodomy, divorce, suicides or gang fights may be limited almost entirely to that one particular area that is now ruled by these spirits.

We have noticed in the news how a rapist or strangler will seem to be limited to a particular area. In Kansas City, there is one area with a radius of five blocks where, in the space of a year, nineteen rapes were reported. Investigation revealed that in the days when people were migrating west, this was an area where there were a lot of saloons and all the accompanying sins of the Wild West. It is an area in which it has proven very difficult to have a revival or to establish a ministry. In such areas, Satan puts a barrier over people's minds and causes much oppression. You will usually find a great deal of fighting and discord among the people of such an area. Even in the existing churches of that area, you will find division, strife, discord, splits and general discontent.

Christians will also have a hard time living an overcoming life in such an atmosphere. They frequently lose their power to witness. Some even live in fear. There are also certain satanic areas where there are repeated fatal car accidents. It is in places like this where revolutionary extremism, such as Naziism and Communism, can make great inroads. Car accidents occur in a place where there is apathy and violence.

When I first arrived in Baton Rouge, I worked at Eden Park Elementary School. On a corner near the school, there was an accident every morning and every afternoon. There was a traffic light on that corner, but in spite of it, accidents continued. Eventually, I realized what was happening, took authority over the spirit of accidents and violence, and I have seen no more accidents there from that day to this.

> ***When the Israelites were living in the land of Goshen, God sent the plagues upon Egypt, but He put a hedge around the land of Goshen, where His people lived!***

Spirits can go so far, but no further than their allotted area. The thing that stops them are the prayers and the holiness of God's people. Prayer cells, praying families, intercessors ... all these positive things serve to keep an area clean from Satan's inroads into it.

By looking at the life of Job, we can see that God marks off the area where His children live. God knows the addresses of those who love Him and, just as Satan said about Job:

> *Hast not thou made an hedge about him, and about his house, and about all that he hath on every side? thou hast blessed the work of his hands, and his substance is increased in the land.* Job 1:10

Even Satan has to recognize God's hedge of protection and blessing.

When the Israelites were living in the land of Goshen, God sent the plagues upon Egypt, but He put a hedge around the land of Goshen, where His people lived. At least five of the ten plagues never touched the children of Israel or their possessions: the flies (see Exodus 8:22-23), the death of the cattle (see Exodus 9:4 and 6), the hail (see Exodus 9:25-26), the darkness (see Exodus 10:21-23) and the death of the firstborn (see Exodus 12:23).

If Satan can place a canopy of evil over an area simply because he has his servants and demons there to work, worship and obey him, then our God certainly can put a canopy of protection, blessing and even glory over His people. He did it for the Israelites in the wilderness on their way to the Promised Land, as He had in Goshen, and that was right there in the midst of Egypt.

How Satan Works and Whom He Attacks

Satan will always zero in on an important area, an important ministry or a special, anointed person. Yes, every great ministry and servant of God will come under satanic attack. Job was a target (see Job 1) and so was David (see 1 Chronicles 21:1). Paul was attacked by a messenger of Satan:

> *There was given to me a thorn in the flesh, the messenger of Satan.* 2 Corinthians 12:7

Some of the Ways Satan Attacks

Satan works to damage the reputation of those in leadership. He brings reproach, and he stirs up jealousies. He sends a spirit of rebellion against leadership and causes insurrection.

He brings confusion through those who speak negatively and critically. He causes sickness, death and accidents. He lies and causes old friends to slander one another.

Through theft of funds in the mail by some of the members of the ministry or organization, he reduces finances. Satan always attacks financially, through the immoral conduct of those in leadership.

One of Satan's masterstrokes is causing false doctrine or half-truths to enter a ministry. Compromise is also a method he uses. When we compromise with evil, we let down the wall of protection.

Through petty nuisances, such as thieves breaking in, pipes bursting, electrical failures, loss of mailing lists, the breakdown of vital machines, fires, etc. And Christians must be very careful not to assist Satan in his attack against other Christians. All too often, we are his most powerful tools.

The sad thing is that when Satan attacks a ministry, very often God's people join him to help destroy that ministry. It seems as though we are too ready to see our brothers fall. We take a delight that is demonically inspired, and we are often too weak and cowardly to stand by the one who is under attack. We sometimes even disassociate ourselves from him.

These are the days of defamation of character, disloyalty, betrayal, greed and self-preservation. If we live a holy life, we certainly will be tested and tried, but we will come through victoriously. If we yield to Satan's attacks and do not withstand him, he will rule the world. James declared:

> *Resist the devil, and he will flee from you.* James 4:7

THE AUTHORITY OF THE BELIEVER OVER DEMON SPIRITS

We can begin to turn things around by joining with other Spirit-filled believers to battle against the enemy of our souls. God said to Ezekiel:

> *And I sought for a man among them, that should make up the hedge, and stand in the gap before me for the land, that I should not destroy it: but I found none. Therefore have I poured out mine indignation upon them; I have consumed them with the fire of my wrath: their own way have I recompensed upon their heads, saith the Lord GOD.* Ezekiel 22:30-31

Sometimes all God needs is one revivalist, one man like Noah who salvaged the adamic race by his righteousness, one Abraham, who was called out of Nimrod's system to begin a new race of people, one Moses, who was saved to lead a nation out of captivity, one Joshua, a young slave delivered out of Egypt and trained by God and Moses to possess the land, one David, a shepherd boy used to redeem Israel from her enemies, one Elijah, used to call a nation back to God, one Isaiah, one Jeremiah or one Ezekiel, used to prophesy and sound the trumpet, one Paul, used to bring the world the message of the Gospel, regeneration by faith in Christ, one Deborah, one Ruth, one Esther, one Abigail, one Hannah, one Anna or one Mary.

The Groundwork

But how do we begin?

1. We must confess our sins and the sins of our nation.
2. We must seek for forgiveness.
3. Jesus sacrifice must be recognized, accepted and appropriated.
4. Satan must be rebuked and reproved and told that Jesus paid the sacrifice of His own blood and that he (Satan) is a usurper.
5. The land is then redeemed by an act of faith which applies the blood of Jesus to the curse. This alone, breaks the power and authority which demons have over our land.

The Scriptures promise:

Much more then, being now justified by his blood, we shall be saved from wrath through him. Romans 5:9

Forasmuch as ye know that ye were not redeemed with corruptible things, as silver and gold, from your vain conversation received by tradition from your fathers; But with the precious blood of Christ, as of a lamb without blemish and without spot. 1 Peter 1:18-19

If God recognized the blood sacrifice of Saul's sons and accepted it as atonement for the sins of their father, how much more readily will He accept the sacrifice of His own Son for the redemption of our land?

BINDING INSTEAD OF DISLODGING THE SPIRITS

Finally, it is important to get the demons out. We keep on binding the devils, when these demons should be rooted out and dislodged. By binding them, we hinder their work, but they must be cast out and dislodged completely before there will be complete deliverance. Binding is only temporary, loosing them from their assignment is permanent.

Take your authority today, and do what needs to be done, for your home, your church, your community, your nation and the world.

The Violent Take It By Force. Will you be one of them?

Ministry Page

You may contact the author at the following addresses:

Prophetess Jackie Harewood
37041 Agnes Webb Avenue
Prarieville, LA 70769

Phone: 225-313-3142
FAX: 223-313-3144

Email: jharewoodla@yahoo.com
www.faithcityinternational.org

Prophetess Jacqueline "Jackie" Harewood's Bio

EDUCATION

- BSW in Social Work from Southern University, Baton Rouge, Louisiana
- Diploma from Spencer College in Business Administration, Accounting, Baton Rouge, Louisiana
- Diploma from Ministers' Training Institute in General Ministries, Karlsruhe, Germany
- Diploma from Northsworthy School of Theology, in Religious Studies, Crailsheim, Germany
- Completed License to Preach School, Louisiana Conference, UMC
- A graduate of Grantsmanship Center, New Orleans. She is a proposal writer and has obtained funding for several grants for non-profit organizations.

EMPLOYMENT

- Part-time Director of Shalom Ministries for the Louisiana Conference, UMC
- Dean of Education and Instructor at International Fellowship of Faith Churches Bible Institute, Baton Rouge, Louisiana
- Affiliate of Campus Crusade for Christ International, Military Ministry Division

MINISTRY

- Has conducted conferences, seminars and evangelistic crusades in North America, Europe and the Caribbean
- Conducts ecumenical conferences on the Holy Spirit and healing services
- Is Coordinator of When Women Pray International (USA Branch)
- Is a prayer consultant (She trains prayer warriors and teaches many prayer groups in denominational and ecumenical groups. She has started intercessory groups in UMC churches and enhanced existing prayer groups with her teaching and activation skills.
- Has conducted spiritual warfare and intercession conferences in the Caribbean, the Islands of the West Indies, Northern Antilles, Europe and North America
- Is featured on television: Channel 20, Saturdays at 9:30 A.M. and Channel 10, Sundays at 9:00 A.M. in the Metropolitan Baton Rouge, Louisiana area

PERSONAL

- Is married to Apostle David Harewood, Pastor of Faith City International Ministries, Baton Rouge, Louisiana
- Has authored several other books and manuals
- Participated in Louisiana Conference, UM Cokesbury book display as an author
- Is a member of the following organizations: Phi Alpha National Social Workers Honor Society, National Association of Social Workers, Student representative to the Board of National Association of Social Workers 2004-2005, International Intercessors

www.ingramcontent.com/pod-product-compliance
Lightning Source LLC
LaVergne TN
LVHW011331080426
835513LV00006B/283

* 9 7 8 1 9 3 4 7 6 9 1 1 9 *